MEMORY

Functional Skills

FUNCTIONAL SKILLS

CATEGORY CROSS-OUT

Category Cross-Out Activity Instructions

Identify the Category: Recognize the category among the four words, e.g., "Fruits."

Spot the Outlier: Find the word that doesn't belong, e.g., "Desk."

Cross Out the Outlier: Mark the odd word, e.g., cross out "Desk."

How This Helps

Enhanced Language Skills: Category cross-out exercises improve language skills by aiding word retrieval, expanding vocabulary, and enhancing overall linguistic abilities.

Cognitive Stimulation: These exercises stimulate categorization, recognition, and logical thinking, contributing to cognitive rehabilitation, memory enhancement, and problem-solving for stroke survivors.

Precise Communication: Accurate categorization improves communication precision, enabling individuals to express themselves clearly in everyday conversations.

Focused Attention: Completing category cross-out activities enhances sustained attention, which is crucial for language comprehension and effective communication, benefiting stroke survivors working on their attention span.

By engaging in these exercises, stroke survivors not only aid in language recovery but also benefit from cognitive stimulation, improved communication precision, and increased confidence in their language skills.

Embark on a transformative journey with "Rewiring My Brain: Activities for Aphasia Rehabilitation," your reliable guide in the path of healing and rediscovery. Each page is a beacon of hope, helping you reclaim the vibrant spectrum of life that aphasia has clouded.

This workbook is an oasis of growth and empowerment, systematically designed to reforge your connection to language and communication through:

💎 Language Section: Deep dive into linguistic nuances with exercises like Category Fill-ins and Cross-outs, and explore synonyms, antonyms, and homonyms to rebuild your language foundation, step by step.

💼 Sentence Structure Exercises: Enhance your ability to construct meaningful sentences with activities focused on phrase and sentence completion, nurturing confidence in your communicative skills.

🧠 Cognitive Section: Revitalize your cognitive abilities with exercises fostering comprehension, general knowledge, and memory retention, paving a path to a sharper and more engaged mind.

Embrace this workbook as a vessel of self-healing, promoting gradual and significant progress. Through each activity, rediscover the joy of articulating thoughts and connecting with the world anew.

Together, let's nurture your mind back to its full potential, one activity at a time. Welcome to your sanctuary of healing and growth.

Disclaimer: This workbook is intended to assist in the recovery from aphasia. However, it is not a replacement for professional medical advice or treatment. Please consult with a healthcare provider for personalized medical advice.

Table of Contents
Language Section

WORDS

SENTENCE STRUCTURE

Cognition Section

COMPREHENSION

GENERAL KNOWLEDGE

Category Cross-out

Identify and out the words that don't belong to the listed categories.

Apple	Giraffe	Elephant	Zebra
Helicopter	Bicycle	Rocket	Airplane
Umbrella	Mercury	Jupiter	Neptune
Jeans	T-shirt	Blouse	Banana
Printer	Mango	Calculator	Scanner
Lion	Alligator	Tiger	Zebra
Car	Flute	Violin	Harp
Yacht	Submarine	Pear	Cruiser
Microwave	Leopard	Tiger	Cheetah
Nebula	Galaxy	Ocean	Comet
Bucket	Aquarium	Bathtub	Sink
Trumpet	Clarinet	Flute	Sofa
Plum	Peach	Apple	Grapefruit
Mountain	Canyon	Valley	Lamp
Wolf	Coyote	Fox	Bicycle
Newspaper	Radio	Magazine	Cat
Oak	Birch	Pine	Chair
Skirt	Dress	Orange	Blouse
Tablet	Laptop	Phone	Grape
Viola	Cello	Airplane	Violin

Category Cross-out

Identify and cross out the words that don't belong to the listed categories.

Guitar	Piano	Drums	Banana
Tea	Coffee	Juice	Book
Winter	Spring	Summer	Chair
Bee	Butterfly	Bird	Fridge
Laptop	Tablet	Smartphone	Grape
Paintbrush	Canvas	Easel	Cat
Carrot	Potato	Tomato	Lamp
Desk	Blackboard	Chalk	Orange
Curtain	Window	Door	Melon
Rose	Tulip	Lily	Train
Sofa	Armchair	Table	Fish
Moon	Star	Planet	Spoon
Forest	Jungle	Desert	Kettle
Tiger	Lion	Elephant	Fork
Calculator	Ruler	Compass	Bee
Giraffe	Zebra	Leopard	Cup
Marker	Crayon	Pencil	Dolphin
Broccoli	Spinach	Kale	Hat
Truck	Car	Bus	Strawberry
Grapes	Blueberry	Raspberry	Bench

Category Cross-out

Identify and cross out the words that don't belong to the listed categories.

Sun	Moon	Stars	Socks
Lettuce	Cucumber	Carrot	Violin
Bicycle	Scooter	Motorcycle	Lemon
Dog	Cat	Rabbit	Pillow
Mouse	Keyboard	Monitor	Apple
Library	Bookstore	School	Hammer
Zebra	Elephant	Giraffe	Kettle
Sink	Bathtub	Shower	Banana
Television	Radio	Newspaper	Tulip
Lizard	Snake	Turtle	Chair
Muffin	Cake	Pie	Grass
Apple	Pear	Peach	Desk
River	Lake	Pond	Lightbulb
Piano	Violin	Flute	Tiger
Sofa	Bed	Wardrobe	Peach
Plate	Bowl	Glass	Turtle
Ant	Bee	Spider	Refrigerator
Laptop	Printer	Scanner	Orange
Basketball	Volleyball	Soccer	Umbrella
Chair	Table	Desk	Butterfly

Category Cross-out

Identify and cross out the words that don't belong to the listed categories.

Peach	Banana	Car	Grape
Dog	Plane	Boat	Bus
Chair	Bird	Desk	Table
Shirt	Fish	Socks	Pants
Flower	Spoon	Knife	Fork
Pencil	Pen	Eraser	Elephant
Basketball	Soccer	Tennis	Lion
Dolphin	Bicycle	Shark	Whale
Fridge	Oven	Microwave	Sun
Moon	Stars	Sky	Horse
River	Lake	Ocean	Tree
Cow	Car	Goat	Sheep
Bread	Butter	Jam	Tiger
Plate	Cup	Glass	Moon
Mountain	Hill	Pen	Valley
Window	Door	Wall	Frog
Rug	Carpet	Tile	Apple
Lamp	Light	Chandelier	Butterfly
Mango	Chair	Lemon	Orange
Notebook	Paper	Clipboard	Dolphin

Category Cross-out

Identify and cross out the words that don't belong to the listed categories.

Army	Navy	Grapes	Marines
Triangle	Square	Circle	Dolphin
Piano	Guitar	Drums	Mountain
Lion	Tiger	Elephant	Microscope
Mercury	Venus	Mars	Bicycle
Football	Baseball	Cricket	Telescope
Rose	Tulip	Lily	Refrigerator
Sparrow	Eagle	Robin	Envelope
Bee	Butterfly	Moth	Sandwich
Winter	Summer	Spring	Aquarium
Jazz	Rock	Blues	Television
Ruby	Emerald	Sapphire	Motorcycle
Fridge	Oven	Microwave	Lighthouse
Oak	Pine	Birch	Submarine
Spain	France	Italy	Carrot
Comedy	Tragedy	Drama	Aeroplane
Hippo	Crocodile	Elephant	Fountain
Romeo	Juliet	Othello	Spaceship
Jupiter	Mars	Neptune	Sheriff
Ocean	Sea	River	Telephone

Category Cross-out

Identify and cross out the words that don't belong to the listed categories.

Giraffe	Bicycle	Elephant	Gazelle
Trumpet	Mango	Guitar	Violin
Mars	Shovel	Jupiter	Saturn
Blueberry	Laptop	Strawberry	Raspberry
Flute	Carrot	Pepper	Broccoli
Piano	Cucumber	Clarinet	Flugelhorn
Football	Boat	Soccer	Basketball
Cough	Fever	Headache	Tablet
Car	Boat	Giraffe	Plane
Symphony	Opera	Newspaper	Ballet
Compass	Window	Calculator	Protractor
Venus	Guitar	Mercury	Earth
Shark	Whale	Mountain	Dolphin
Rose	Television	Dandelion	Tulip
Octopus	Laptop	Jellyfish	Squid
Daffodil	Lily	Balloon	Orchid
Penne	Chicken	Ravioli	Spaghetti
Gouda	Brie	Cheddar	Skyscraper
Monitor	Keyboard	Telephone	Mouse
Mercedes	Toyota	Honda	Cupcake

Category Cross-out

Identify and cross out the words that don't belong to the listed categories.

Tiger	Elephant	Zebra	Microphone
Violin	Flute	Trumpet	Grapefruit
Fan	Mars	Jupiter	Saturn
Raspberry	Laptop	Mango	Blueberry
Harp	Strawberry	Guitar	Flute
Cucumber	Broccoli	Carrot	Drum
Computer	Volleyball	Football	Basketball
Headache	Cold	Cough	Skyscraper
Drama	Carrot	Musical	Comedy
Hexagon	Circle	Triangle	Flute
Paperclip	Scissors	Stapler	Shark
Venus	Neptune	Violin	Earth
Computer	Shark	Dolphin	Whale
Sunflower	Daisy	Tulip	Printer
Squid	Crab	Shrimp	Keyboard
Daffodil	Lily	Tulip	Aeroplane
Linguine	Spaghetti	Television	Penne
Camembert	Gouda	Roquefort	Ship
Printer	Banana	Keyboard	Mouse
Blueberry	Honda	Ford	Lexus

Category Cross-out

Identify and cross out the words that don't belong to the listed categories.

Rhino	Leopard	Hippopotamus	Orchestra
Tuba	Flugelhorn	Piccolo	Sparrow
Pluto	Saturn	Venus	Croissant
Mango	Papaya	Guava	Tractor
Xylophone	Marimba	Drum	Algebra
Zucchini	Cucumber	Cauliflower	Guitar
Badminton	Hockey	Football	Butterfly
Sinusitis	Asthma	Bronchitis	Guitar
Tragedy	Romance	Thriller	Sunflower
Dodecagon	Heptagon	Octagon	Marimba
Stapler	Clipboard	Calculator	Giraffe
Saturn	Neptune	Uranus	Banjo
Porpoise	Seal	Manatee	Printer
Begonia	Hyacinth	Iris	Telescope
Jellyfish	Starfish	Cuttlefish	Drumset
Violet	Tulip	Rose	Aircraft
Fusilli	Gnocchi	Penne	Submarine
Gorgonzola	Cheddar	Feta	Aeroplane
Scanner	Projector	Router	Gazelle
Kia	Volvo	Mercedes	Lilac

Category Cross-out

Identify and cross out the words that don't belong to the listed categories.

Mongoose	Chimpanzee	Gorilla	Flamenco
Oboe	Cornet	Bassoon	Dolphin
Mercury	Uranus	Jupiter	Strawberry
Apricot	Kiwi	Cherry	Bicycle
Harpsichord	Cello	Viola	Pyramid
Artichoke	Asparagus	Spinach	Bassoon
Squash	Volleyball	Badminton	Butterfly
Laryngitis	Gastritis	Arthritis	Kettle
Noir	Romcom	Drama	Cactus
Nonagon	Decagon	Hexagon	Violin
Compass	Ruler	Protractor	Mango
Neptune	Mars	Earth	Harpsichord
Narwhal	Manatee	Seahorse	Telescope
Peony	Geranium	Lavender	Car
Sardine	Anchovy	Herring	Computer
Aster	Carnation	Tulip	Aeroplane
Tagliatelle	Cavatappi	Farfalle	Biplane
Havarti	Brie	Roquefort	Scooter
Modem	Harddrive	Router	Orchid
Tesla	Maserati	Bentley	Sunflower

Category Cross-out

Identify and cross out the words that don't belong to the listed categories.

Ballet	Humpback	Seahorse	Orca
Castle	Trumpet	Violin	Trombone
Hyena	Accordion	Gazelle	Elephant
Harmonica	Cheetah	Panther	Lion
Glockenspiel	Marimba	Xylophone	Cheetah
Lily	Tulip	Hyacinth	Soccer
Cricket	Lily	Football	Soccer
Meningitis	Tonsillitis	Guitar	Bronchitis
Bassoon	Melodrama	Comedy	Tragedy
Icosagon	Trombone	Octagon	Dodecagon
Pliers	Screwdriver	Wrench	Orca
Jaguar	BMW	Saxophone	Tesla
Walrus	Seal	Narwhal	Violin
Azalea	Begonia	Carnation	Cricket
Basketball	Mackerel	Herring	Anchovy
Zinnia	Petunia	Football	Moon
Linguini	Tortellini	Ravioli	Glockenspiel
Feta	Baseball	Mozzarella	Gouda
Router	Modem	Scanner	Dolphin
Audi	Melodrma	Infiniti	Toyota

Category Cross-out

Identify and cross out the words that don't belong to the listed categories.

Apple	Motorcycle	Orange	Grape
Car	Elephant	Dog	Lion
Blue	Red	Truck	Green
Bicycle	Airplane	Strawberry	Bus
Cherry	Banana	Ship	Peach
Tiger	Train	Giraffe	Cat
Black	Yellow	Wolf	White
Scooter	Boat	Orange	Motorcycle
Melon	Horse	Lemon	Kiwi
Zebra	Bear	Blue	Monkey
Silver	Pink	Bullet	Maroon
Helicopter	Truck	Subway	Car
Watermelon	Apple	Bicycle	Raspberry
Dolphin	Elephant	Train	Snake
Green	Indigo	Tesla	Red
Yacht	Jet Ski	Rocket	Grape
Plum	Mango	Fan	Pear
Cow	Dog	Lion	Frog
Olive	Teal	Violet	Barn

CATEGORY FILL-INS

Category Fill-In Section Instructions

Objective: To categorize words, enhancing word recognition and categorization skills, especially beneficial for individuals with aphasia.

How This Exercise Helps:
This categorization task aids people with aphasia by reinforcing their ability to recognize and sort words into categories. It helps in improving cognitive processing, particularly in the areas of organization and association, which are crucial for effective communication.

How to Use:
Review the Word List: Start by looking at the 30 random words provided at the top of the page.

Understand the Categories: Below the word list, you will find six categories for sorting.

Sort the Words: Carefully read each word and decide which category it belongs to.

Place Each Word Correctly: Write or type each word under the appropriate category. Some words may seem like they fit in more than one category, so use your best judgment.

Review Your Work: Once all words are categorized, review your choices. Consider why each word fits in its category.

Tip: Don't rush; take your time to think about each word and its meaning. If unsure, make your best guess and move on. You can always come back to it. It's okay to ask for help or use resources like a dictionary. Remember, the goal is to practice and improve at your own pace.

Category Fill-Ins

Fill in each blank in the category grid with one word from the list below, ensuring each word correctly corresponds to its category.

Sofa	Mango	Blue	Sydney	Flute
Vacuum	Broccoli	Violin	Paris	Sparrow
Piano	Green	Elephant	Tokyo	Baguette
Refrigerator	Kangaroo	Yellow	Microwave	Mumbai
Drums	Toronto	Lamp	Red	Giraffe
Guitar	Pasta	Salmon	Violet	Dolphin

ANIMALS

1. _______________________
2. _______________________
3. _______________________
4. _______________________
5. _______________________

FOODS

1. _______________________
2. _______________________
3. _______________________
4. _______________________
5. _______________________

CITIES

1. _______________________
2. _______________________
3. _______________________
4. _______________________
5. _______________________

MUSICAL INSTRUMENTS

1. _______________________
2. _______________________
3. _______________________
4. _______________________
5. _______________________

HOUSEHOLD ITEMS

1. _______________________
2. _______________________
3. _______________________
4. _______________________
5. _______________________

COLORS

1. _______________________
2. _______________________
3. _______________________
4. _______________________
5. _______________________

Category Fill-Ins

Fill in each blank in the category grid with one word from the list below, ensuring each word correctly corresponds to its category.

Ford	Canada	Toaster	Marigold	Volleyball
Basketball	Hockey	BMW	Orchid	River
Ocean	Tulip	Japan	Refrigerator	Mercedes
Brazil	Pond	Soccer	Toyota	Microwave
Lake	Blender	Germany	Daffodil	Baseball
Spain	Oven	Rose	Honda	Stream

FLOWERS

1. _______________________
2. _______________________
3. _______________________
4. _______________________
5. _______________________

CAR BRANDS

1. _______________________
2. _______________________
3. _______________________
4. _______________________
5. _______________________

COUNTRIES

1. _______________________
2. _______________________
3. _______________________
4. _______________________
5. _______________________

BODIES OF WATER

1. _______________________
2. _______________________
3. _______________________
4. _______________________
5. _______________________

KITCHEN APPLIANCES

1. _______________________
2. _______________________
3. _______________________
4. _______________________
5. _______________________

SPORTS

1. _______________________
2. _______________________
3. _______________________
4. _______________________
5. _______________________

Category Fill-Ins

Fill in each blank in the category grid with one word from the list below, ensuring each word correctly corresponds to its category.

Green	Mango	Chair	Giraffe	Motorcycle
Sofa	Yellow	Iron	Cherry	Airplane
Zinc	Blue	Sparrow	Dresser	Car
Table	Red	Gold	Elephant	Banana
Copper	Violet	Apple	Bicycle	Kangaroo
Silver	Wardrobe	Truck	Grape	Dolphin

VEHICLES

1. _______________
2. _______________
3. _______________
4. _______________
5. _______________

METALS

1. _______________
2. _______________
3. _______________
4. _______________
5. _______________

FURNITURE

1. _______________
2. _______________
3. _______________
4. _______________
5. _______________

COLORS

1. _______________
2. _______________
3. _______________
4. _______________
5. _______________

FRUITS

1. _______________
2. _______________
3. _______________
4. _______________
5. _______________

ANIMALS

1. _______________
2. _______________
3. _______________
4. _______________
5. _______________

Category Fill-Ins

Fill in each blank in the category grid with one word from the list below, ensuring each word correctly corresponds to its category.

Sunny	Pentagon	Flute	Kitchen	Sneakers
Snowy	Square	Piano	Bedroom	Heels
January	Circle	Guitar	March	Living Room
Triangle	Drums	Rainy	Bathroom	Sandals
Windy	February	May	Loafers	Dinning Room
Cloudy	Rectangle	Violin	April	Boots

MONTHS

1. _______________
2. _______________
3. _______________
4. _______________
5. _______________

TYPES OF SHOES

1. _______________
2. _______________
3. _______________
4. _______________
5. _______________

ROOM TYPES

1. _______________
2. _______________
3. _______________
4. _______________
5. _______________

MUSICAL INSTRUMENTS

1. _______________
2. _______________
3. _______________
4. _______________
5. _______________

SHAPES

1. _______________
2. _______________
3. _______________
4. _______________
5. _______________

WEATHER CONDITIONS

1. _______________
2. _______________
3. _______________
4. _______________
5. _______________

Category Fill-Ins

Fill in each blank in the category grid with one word from the list below, ensuring each word correctly corresponds to its category.

Dolphin	Chef	Helicopter	Gold	Sushi
Drum	Almond	Astronaut	Lavender	Elephant
Flute	Piano	Charcoal	Gardener	Avocado
Yacht	Architect	Scooter	Crimson	Kangaroo
Teacher	Turquoise	Violin	Python	Train
Pancake	Bicycle	Guitar	Sparrow	Spaghetti

ANIMALS

1. ___________
2. ___________
3. ___________
4. ___________
5. ___________

COLORS

1. ___________
2. ___________
3. ___________
4. ___________
5. ___________

FOODS

1. ___________
2. ___________
3. ___________
4. ___________
5. ___________

TRANSPORT

1. ___________
2. ___________
3. ___________
4. ___________
5. ___________

OCCUPACTIONS

1. ___________
2. ___________
3. ___________
4. ___________
5. ___________

MUSICAL INSTRUMENTS

1. ___________
2. ___________
3. ___________
4. ___________
5. ___________

Category Fill-Ins

Fill in each blank in the category grid with one word from the list below, ensuring each word correctly corresponds to its category.

Spatula	Finch	Sapphire	Turmeric	Shark
Emerald	Linen	Whisk	Dolphin	Silk
Ladle	Cinnamon	Octopus	Topaz	Robin
Satin	Clove	Diamond	Eagle	Cotton
Denim	Seahorse	Pigeon	Grater	Ginger
Tongs	Jellyfish	Sparrow	Paprika	Ruby

GEMSTONES

1. _______________
2. _______________
3. _______________
4. _______________
5. _______________

KITCHEN UTENSILS

1. _______________
2. _______________
3. _______________
4. _______________
5. _______________

BIRDS

1. _______________
2. _______________
3. _______________
4. _______________
5. _______________

TYPES OF FABRIC

1. _______________
2. _______________
3. _______________
4. _______________
5. _______________

SPICES

1. _______________
2. _______________
3. _______________
4. _______________
5. _______________

OCEAN CREATURES

1. _______________
2. _______________
3. _______________
4. _______________
5. _______________

Category Fill-Ins

Fill in each blank in the category grid with one word from the list below, ensuring each word correctly corresponds to its category.

Souffle	Mystery	Beetle	Mosquito	Comet
Dragonfly	Baseball	Gelato	Silver	Thriller
Palladium	Butterfly	Cricket	Gold	Cupcake
Rhodium	Tiramisu	Animation	Soccer	Asteroid
Volleyball	Meteor	Brownie	Romance	Nebula
Grasshopper	Platinum	Galaxy	Documenary	Basketball

SPORTS

1. _______________
2. _______________
3. _______________
4. _______________
5. _______________

FILM GENRES

1. _______________
2. _______________
3. _______________
4. _______________
5. _______________

DESSERTS

1. _______________
2. _______________
3. _______________
4. _______________
5. _______________

PRECIOUS METALS

1. _______________
2. _______________
3. _______________
4. _______________
5. _______________

INSECTS

1. _______________
2. _______________
3. _______________
4. _______________
5. _______________

SPACE BODIES

1. _______________
2. _______________
3. _______________
4. _______________
5. _______________

Category Fill-Ins

Fill in each blank in the category grid with one word from the list below, ensuring each word correctly corresponds to its category.

Dali	Fusilli	Calculator	Brick	Everest
Gypsum	Baroque	Envelope	Highlighter	Elbrus
Penne	Ancient	Kilimanjaro	Clipboard	Fuji
Renaissance	Monet	Linguine	Rebar	Picasso
VanGogh	Farfalle	Stapler	Plywood	McKinley
Medieval	Cement	Rotini	Victorian	Rembrandt

MOUNTAINS

1.
2.
3.
4.
5.

TYPES OF PASTA

1.
2.
3.
4.
5.

OFFICE SUPPLIES

1.
2.
3.
4.
5.

PERIODS OF HISTORY

1.
2.
3.
4.
5.

CONSTRUCTION MATERIALS

1.
2.
3.
4.
5.

FAMOUS ARTISTS

1.
2.
3.
4.
5.

Category Fill-Ins

Fill in each blank in the category grid with one word from the list below, ensuring each word correctly corresponds to its category.

Legato	Brooch	Tango	Crescendo	Cream
Butter	America	Earrings	Chemistry	Ballet
Staccato	Geology	Bracelet	Astronomy	Antarctica
Africa	Yogurt	Salsa	Milk	Ring
Waltz	Physics	Asia	Allegro	Forte
Europe	Necklace	Cheese	Hip-hop	Biology

CONTINENTS

1. _______________________
2. _______________________
3. _______________________
4. _______________________
5. _______________________

MUSICAL TERMS

1. _______________________
2. _______________________
3. _______________________
4. _______________________
5. _______________________

PIECES OF JEWELRY

1. _______________________
2. _______________________
3. _______________________
4. _______________________
5. _______________________

TYPES OF DANCES

1. _______________________
2. _______________________
3. _______________________
4. _______________________
5. _______________________

BRANCHES OF SCIENCE

1. _______________________
2. _______________________
3. _______________________
4. _______________________
5. _______________________

DAIRY PRODUCTS

1. _______________________
2. _______________________
3. _______________________
4. _______________________
5. _______________________

Category Fill-Ins

Fill in each blank in the category grid with one word from the list below, ensuring each word correctly corresponds to its category.

Tesla	Oxygen	Beret	Plato	Basil
Trilby	Fedora	BMW	Nietzsche	Gymnastics
Swimming	Fencing	Toyota	Aristotle	Oregano
Rowing	Carbon	Rosemary	Socrates	Beanie
Thyme	Hydrogen	Kant	Ford	Gold
Mint	Sombrero	Honda	Silver	Archery

KITCHEN HERBS

1.
2.
3.
4.
5.

OLYMPIC SPORTS

1.
2.
3.
4.
5.

CAR BRANDS

1.
2.
3.
4.
5.

TYPES OF HATS

1.
2.
3.
4.
5.

ELEMENTS ON THE PERIODIC TABLE

1.
2.
3.
4.
5.

FAMOUS PHILOSOPHERS

1.
2.
3.
4.
5.

Category Fill-Ins

Fill in each blank in the category grid with one word from the list below, ensuring each word correctly corresponds to its category.

Apple	Doctor	River	Poetry	Salad
Library	Rain	Lawyer	Train	Music
Courage	Guitar	Rose	Movie	Tiger
Basketball	Friendship	Mathematics	Ocean	School
Elephant	Computer	Lion	Baker	Painting
Blue	Happiness	Car	Red	Sunshine

FRUITS & VEGETABLES

1.
2.
3.
4.
5.

PROFESSIONS

1.
2.
3.
4.
5.

NATURE & ENVIRONMENT

1.
2.
3.
4.
5.

FEELINGS & EMOTIONS

1.
2.
3.
4.
5.

ANIMALS & WILDLIFE

1.
2.
3.
4.
5.

ARTS & ENTERTAINMENT

1.
2.
3.
4.
5.

CONVERGENT NAMING

Convergent Naming Activity Instructions

Objective:
Enhance word retrieval and strengthen categorization skills, aiding language rehabilitation in individuals with aphasia.

How This Exercise Helps:
Word Retrieval: Assists in recalling and using words.

Categorization: Improves organizing and grouping words.

Associative Thinking: Enhances connections between related words.

Confidence Building: Boosts self-assurance in language abilities.

How to Use:
Read Words: View the list (e.g., "waves, surf, sand, seashells, coastal") and visualize each.

Identify Category: Determine the common theme linking the words (e.g., beach-related items).

Fill in the Blank: Add a word that fits the theme, either written or spoken (e.g., "ocean").

Reflect: Think about how the words interconnect and explore other potential categories they may fit.

Tip: Encourage patience and repetition. If initially challenging, repeat words or use visual aids. Celebrate small successes to build confidence.

Convergent Naming

Using the clues provided in each row, identify and write down the common object or concept they are describing.

Hops... Malt... Fermented... Pint... Brewery... _______________

Large... Trunk... Grey... Tusks... Herbivore... _______________

Feathers... Flight... Nest... Tweets... Aviary... _______________

Roots... Trunk... Leaves... Photosynthesis... Shade... _______________

Keyboard... Monitor... Cpu... Mouse... Software... _______________

Mountains... Rivers... Continents... Oceans... Planet... _______________

Lava... Eruption... Magma... Crater... Ash... _______________

White... Puffy... Sky... Float... Shapes... _______________

Sails... Anchor... Sea... Captain... Voyage... _______________

Yellow... Ripe... Peel... Fruit... Monkey's Favorite... _______________

Strings... Frets... Strum... Melody... Acoustic... _______________

Wings... Takeoff... Cockpit... Altitude... Passengers... _______________

Beats... Melody... Lyrics... Album... Artist... _______________

Bright... Hot... Rises In The East... Solar... Star... _______________

Dew... Petals... Garden... Bloom... Fragrance... _______________

Gills... Scales... Fins... Aquatic... Swimmers... _______________

Frozen... Icicles... Snowflakes... Cold... Season... _______________

Whiskers... Fur... Meows... Purrs... Feline... _______________

Eight Legs... Web... Arachnid... Spins... Crawls... _______________

Sweet... Hive... Bees... Golden... Nectar... _______________

Convergent Naming

Using the clues provided in each row, identify and write down the common object or concept they are describing.

Green... Photosynthesis... Chlorophyll... Stems... Flora... _______________

Ivory Keys... Pedals... Chords... Concert... Grand... _______________

Milky Way... Celestial... Planets... Orbit... Astronomy... _______________

Waves... Surf... Sand... Seashells... Coastal... _______________

Pages... Chapters... Cover... Literature... Reading... _______________

Orbit... Gravitational Pull... Lunar... Craters... Night Sky... _______________

Reptile... Scales... Cold-blooded... Slithers... Venom... _______________

Caffeine... Brew... Arabica... Espresso... Morning Beverage... _______________

Hoops... Dribble... Court... Slam Dunk... Basketball... _______________

Frets... Strings... Bow... Concert... Classical... _______________

Needles... Thread... Fabric... Patterns... Sewing... _______________

Canvas... Brush... Palette... Strokes... Gallery... _______________

Cylinders... Engine... Wheels... Drive... Transportation... _______________

Amphibian... Webbed Feet... Jumps... Pond... Ribbit... _______________

Equine... Saddle... Gallop... Mane... Stable... _______________

H2o... Hydration... Liquid... Fountain... Refreshment... _______________

Spherical... Bounce... Dribble... Court... Slam Dunk... _______________

Spotlight... Script... Stage... Actors... Drama... _______________

Coils... Voltage... Current... Circuit... Electronics... _______________

Beats... Spinning... Headphones... Track... Disc Jockey... _______________

Convergent Naming

Using the clues provided in each row, identify and write down the common object or concept they are describing.

Shutter... Lens... Focus... Snapshots... Aperture... _______________

Whisk... Oven... Batter... Recipe... Baking... _______________

Antennae... Wings... Hive... Buzz... Pollination... _______________

Stethoscope... White Coat... Patient... Clinic... Physician... _______________

Fins... Snorkel... Coral... Underwater... Scuba... _______________

Sprint... Marathon... Race... Jog... Athletics... _______________

Symphony... Conductor... Orchestra... Instruments... Classical... _______________

Pages... Author... Chapters... Novel... Literature... _______________

Experiment... Beakers... Lab... Chemicals... Science... _______________

Aisle... Ceremony... Bride... Vows... Wedding... _______________

Fur... Paws... Whiskers... Pet... Canine... _______________

Bricks... Mortar... Blueprint... Construction... Building... _______________

Spices... Stove... Recipe... Culinary... Kitchen... _______________

Melody... Harmony... Notes... Rhythm... Music... _______________

Prism... Spectrum... Light... Colors... Rainbow... _______________

Court... Judge... Jury... Trial... Legal... _______________

Meteorologist... Forecast... Clouds... Weather... Prediction... _______________

Microscope... Cells... Biology... Research... Laboratory... _______________

Hooves... Mane... Stallion... Equestrian... Horse... _______________

Nebula... Galaxy... Stars... Space... Cosmos... _______________

Convergent Naming

Using the clues provided in each row, identify and write down the common object or concept they are describing.

Whiskers... Mice... Cheese... Rodent... Squeak... _______________

Stalk... Green... Ears... Husk... Agriculture... _______________

Axis... Globe... Continents... Geographical... Map... _______________

Beak... Feathers... Flight... Aviary... Chirp... _______________

Fermented Grapes... Bottle... Cork... Vineyard... Sommelier... _______________

Reeds... Symphony... Blow... Orchestra... Woodwind... _______________

Canvas... Easel... Strokes... Gallery... Acrylic... _______________

Green... Putt... Course... Hole... Golf... _______________

Solids... Liquids... Gases... Atoms... Chemistry... _______________

Wings... Buzz... Larvae... Insects... Antennae... _______________

Nutrients... Soil... Growth... Garden... Horticulture... _______________

Flicker... Flame... Wick... Melt... Candle... _______________

Scales... Notes... Keys... Piano... Composer... _______________

Paws... Claws... Roar... Mane... Feline... _______________

Racket... Net... Serve... Volley... Tennis... _______________

Alloy... Forge... Anvil... Blacksmith... Metal... _______________

Volume... Chapters... Read... Library... Book... _______________

Stratosphere... Ozone... Sky... Meteorology... Atmosphere... _______________

Vortex... Twirl... Cyclone... Meteorology... Whirlwind... _______________

Gears... Pedal... Cycle... Helmet... Bicycle... _______________

Convergent Naming

Using the clues provided in each row, identify and write down the common object or concept they are describing.

Dew... Petals... Bloom... Fragrance... Horticulture... ________________

Lunar... Phases... Night Sky... Crater... Celestial... ________________

Quantum... Atoms... Particles... Physics... Molecules... ________________

Marinate... Grill... Tender... Culinary... Barbecue... ________________

Hatchling... Feathers... Nest... Ornithology... Bird... ________________

Propeller... Flight... Cockpit... Aviation... Airplane... ________________

Stamen... Pollen... Petals... Botany... Flower... ________________

Oar... Current... River... Nautical... Boat... ________________

Saddle... Stallion... Gallop... Equestrian... Horse... ________________

Decibel... Sound... Vibration... Acoustics... Noise... ________________

Brush... Canvas... Pigment... Artistry... Paint... ________________

Kernel... Butter... Pop... Snack... Popcorn... ________________

Spindle... Thread... Textile... Weave... Fabric... ________________

Lens... Shutter... Photography... Snapshot... Camera... ________________

Stove... Simmer... Culinary... Recipe... Cooking... ________________

Glacier... Icy... Polar... Geology... Frozen... ________________

Tusk... Trunk... Herbivore... Safari... Elephant... ________________

Sashimi... Roll... Nori... Cuisine... Sushi... ________________

Greenhouse... Plants... Horticulture... Flora... Garden... ________________

Telescope... Celestial... Astronomy... Planets... Stargazing... ________________

DIVERGENT NAMING

Divergent Naming Activity

Objective:
To enhance creative thinking and word generation skills by encouraging the production of multiple words within a given category.

How This Exercise Helps:
Creative Thinking: Stimulates the brain to think outside the box and generate diverse words.

Word Generation: Improves the ability to produce a variety of words, enhancing language fluency.

Cognitive Flexibility: Encourages mental flexibility and the ability to shift between different aspects of a category.

Language Expansion: Aids in expanding vocabulary and language expression.

How to Use:
Choose a Category: Pick one from the provided categories, like "Colors."

Generate Words: In the five blank lines, list as many words as you can that are related to the selected category.

Think Creatively: Aim for variety and uniqueness. For "Colors," you might list "red, blue, green, yellow, purple."

Tip: Encourage exploration beyond the obvious. Challenge to think of less common or more abstract words within the category. Emphasize that there are no wrong answers in this creative exercis

Divergent Naming

List five items that belong to each category provided in the spaces below.

FARM ANIMALS

1. ______________________________
2. ______________________________
3. ______________________________
4. ______________________________
5. ______________________________

FRUIT

1. ______________________________
2. ______________________________
3. ______________________________
4. ______________________________
5. ______________________________

CLOTHES

1. ______________________________
2. ______________________________
3. ______________________________
4. ______________________________
5. ______________________________

WOMEN'S NAMES

1. ______________________________
2. ______________________________
3. ______________________________
4. ______________________________
5. ______________________________

AMERICAN CITIES

1. ______________________________
2. ______________________________
3. ______________________________
4. ______________________________
5. ______________________________

TYPES OF PLANTS

1. ______________________________
2. ______________________________
3. ______________________________
4. ______________________________
5. ______________________________

THINGS TO DRINK

1. ______________________________
2. ______________________________
3. ______________________________
4. ______________________________
5. ______________________________

FURNITURE

1. ______________________________
2. ______________________________
3. ______________________________
4. ______________________________
5. ______________________________

Divergent Naming

List five items that belong to each category provided in the spaces below.

MUSICAL INSTRUMENTS
1. _____________________
2. _____________________
3. _____________________
4. _____________________
5. _____________________

FAMOUS BANDS
1. _____________________
2. _____________________
3. _____________________
4. _____________________
5. _____________________

VEGETABLES
1. _____________________
2. _____________________
3. _____________________
4. _____________________
5. _____________________

BODIES OF WATER
1. _____________________
2. _____________________
3. _____________________
4. _____________________
5. _____________________

TYPES OF SHOES
1. _____________________
2. _____________________
3. _____________________
4. _____________________
5. _____________________

AUTHORS
1. _____________________
2. _____________________
3. _____________________
4. _____________________
5. _____________________

MEN'S NAMES
1. _____________________
2. _____________________
3. _____________________
4. _____________________
5. _____________________

KITCHEN APPLIANCES
1. _____________________
2. _____________________
3. _____________________
4. _____________________
5. _____________________

Divergent Naming

List five items that belong to each category provided in the spaces below.

SPORTS TEAMS

1. _______________________________
2. _______________________________
3. _______________________________
4. _______________________________
5. _______________________________

SONG NAMES

1. _______________________________
2. _______________________________
3. _______________________________
4. _______________________________
5. _______________________________

BIRDS

1. _______________________________
2. _______________________________
3. _______________________________
4. _______________________________
5. _______________________________

CAR BRANDS

1. _______________________________
2. _______________________________
3. _______________________________
4. _______________________________
5. _______________________________

MOVIE TITLES

1. _______________________________
2. _______________________________
3. _______________________________
4. _______________________________
5. _______________________________

FAMOUS ARTISTS

1. _______________________________
2. _______________________________
3. _______________________________
4. _______________________________
5. _______________________________

NAMES OF FORMER PRESIDENTS

1. _______________________________
2. _______________________________
3. _______________________________
4. _______________________________
5. _______________________________

DESERTS

1. _______________________________
2. _______________________________
3. _______________________________
4. _______________________________
5. _______________________________

Divergent Naming

List five items that belong to each category provided in the spaces below.

COLORS

1. ______________________
2. ______________________
3. ______________________
4. ______________________
5. ______________________

TYPES OF FLOWERS

1. ______________________
2. ______________________
3. ______________________
4. ______________________
5. ______________________

NAMES OF CEREALS

1. ______________________
2. ______________________
3. ______________________
4. ______________________
5. ______________________

CELEBRITIES

1. ______________________
2. ______________________
3. ______________________
4. ______________________
5. ______________________

TYPES OF BIRDS

1. ______________________
2. ______________________
3. ______________________
4. ______________________
5. ______________________

BOOK GENRES

1. ______________________
2. ______________________
3. ______________________
4. ______________________
5. ______________________

US STATES

1. ______________________
2. ______________________
3. ______________________
4. ______________________
5. ______________________

NAMES OF GIRLS

1. ______________________
2. ______________________
3. ______________________
4. ______________________
5. ______________________

Divergent Naming

List five items that belong to each category provided in the spaces below.

BODY PARTS

1. _______________________________
2. _______________________________
3. _______________________________
4. _______________________________
5. _______________________________

SHAPES

1. _______________________________
2. _______________________________
3. _______________________________
4. _______________________________
5. _______________________________

RESTAURANT NAMES

1. _______________________________
2. _______________________________
3. _______________________________
4. _______________________________
5. _______________________________

DESSERTS

1. _______________________________
2. _______________________________
3. _______________________________
4. _______________________________
5. _______________________________

PIZZA TOPPINGS

1. _______________________________
2. _______________________________
3. _______________________________
4. _______________________________
5. _______________________________

CLOTHES YOU WEAR

1. _______________________________
2. _______________________________
3. _______________________________
4. _______________________________
5. _______________________________

FAMOUS LANDMARKS

1. _______________________________
2. _______________________________
3. _______________________________
4. _______________________________
5. _______________________________

CITIES

1. _______________________________
2. _______________________________
3. _______________________________
4. _______________________________
5. _______________________________

SYNONYMS

Exercise: Sentence Creation with Synonyms

Objective: To enhance creative language use and reinforce understanding of synonyms.

How This Exercise Helps: This exercise encourages individuals with aphasia to actively use their vocabulary, focusing on synonyms, in a sentence. It helps with language fluency and word retrieval.

Instructions:

1. For each word, think of a synonym (a word with a similar meaning).

2. Use the synonym in a sentence.

3. Write your sentence in the space provided.

Example: Joyful
Synonym: Happy
Sentence: The happy child played in the park.

Tip: If you struggle to think of a synonym, consider a context where you might use the word. Create simple sentences; focus on using the synonym correctly. If a word is challenging, skip it and return to it later. Feel free to ask for help or use resources like a thesaurus if needed.

Synonyms

For each word given, create a sentence using a synonym of the word instead of the word itself.

Happy: ____

Fast: ____

Lovely: ____

Mighty: ____

Silent: ____

Clever: ____

Small: ____

Cold: ____

Soft: ____

Bright: ____

Difficult: ____

Thin: ____

Young: ____

Old: ____

Funny: ____

Rich: ____

Calm: ____

Brave: ____

Neat: ____

Lazy: ____

Synonyms

For each word given, create a sentence using a synonym of the word instead of the word itself.

Warm: ____

Wise: ____

Humorous: ____

Tranquil: ____

Courageous: ____

Wealthy: ____

Tidy: ____

Energetic: ____

Tiny: ____

Chilly: ____

Gentle: ____

Luminous: ____

Narrow: ____

Elderly: ____

Complicated: ____

Youthful: ____

Fragile: ____

Dull: ____

Dirty: ____

Loud: ____

Synonyms

For each word give, create a sentence using a synonym of the word instead of the word itself.

Enormous: ____

Hilarious: ____

Serene: ____

Fearless: ____

Opulent: ____

Orderly: ____

Lively: ____

Minute: ____

Freezing: ____

Delicate: ____

Intelligent: ____

Shimmering: ____

Broad: ____

Adolescent: ____

Intricate: ____

Ancient: ____

Sturdy: ____

Filthy: ____

Noisy: ____

Damp: ____

Synonyms

For each word give, create a sentence using a synonym of the word instead of the word itself.

Hefty: ____

Exquisite: ____

Bustling: ____

Parched: ____

Jubilant: ____

Slender: ____

Sprawling: ____

Melancholy: ____

Arid: ____

Flamboyant: ____

Pristine: ____

Frigid: ____

Vast: ____

Petite: ____

Vibrant: ____

Tedious: ____

Soaring: ____

Cluttered: ____

Hushed: ____

Crisp: ____

Synonyms

For each word give, create a sentence using a synonym of the word instead of the word itself.

Joyful: ____

Quickly: ____

Strong: ____

Smart: ____

Old: ____

Happy: ____

Friend: ____

Scared: ____

Tired: ____

Important: ____

Large: ____

Bright: ____

Funny: ____

Thin: ____

Cold: ____

Fast: ____

Rich: ____

Small: ____

Light: ____

SYNONYMS

Exercise: Finding Synonyms

Objective: To match words with their synonyms to improve vocabulary and language flexibility.

How This Exercise Helps: This activity will help you practice recognizing words that have similar meanings, which can aid in language retrieval and usage.

Instructions:

1. Below is a list of words, each paired with a blank line.

2. Your task is to think of a synonym for each word—a word that has the same or a similar meaning.

3. Write the synonym you've thought of on the provided line next to each word.

Example:

Happy: Content   Sad: Unhappy
Fast: Quick   Slow: Leisurely

Synonyms

Find a synonym for each word in the list below and write it on the provided line.

Cosy: _______________________

Serene: _______________________

Subtle: _______________________

Sparse: _______________________

Meager: _______________________

Narrow: _______________________

Keen: _______________________

Mild: _______________________

Rugged: _______________________

Pungent: _______________________

Sincere: _______________________

Vibrant: _______________________

Zestful: _______________________

Dainty: _______________________

Fertile: _______________________

Luminous: _______________________

Pristine: _______________________

Arid: _______________________

Candid: _______________________

Hearty: _______________________

Novel: _______________________

Steady: _______________________

Pliant: _______________________

Balmy: _______________________

Uncomfortable: _______________________

Chaotic: _______________________

Obvious: _______________________

Abundant: _______________________

Plentiful: _______________________

Wide: _______________________

Indifferent: _______________________

Intense: _______________________

Delicate: _______________________

Odorless: _______________________

Insincere: _______________________

Dull: _______________________

Apathetic: _______________________

Clumsy: _______________________

Barren: _______________________

Dim: _______________________

Sullied: _______________________

Damp: _______________________

Evasive: _______________________

Frail: _______________________

Familiar: _______________________

Unstable: _______________________

Rigid: _______________________

Freezing: _______________________

Synonyms

Find a synonym for each word in the list below and write it on the provided line.

Amiable: _____________	Hostile: _____________
Bountiful: _____________	Scarce: _____________
Cherished: _____________	Neglected: _____________
Dauntless: _____________	Timid: _____________
Ephemeral: _____________	Perpetual: _____________
Flourish: _____________	Wither: _____________
Gallant: _____________	Cowardly: _____________
Hilarity: _____________	Gloom: _____________
Immersive: _____________	Superficial: _____________
Jovial: _____________	Sullen: _____________
Kindred: _____________	Unrelated: _____________
Lustrous: _____________	Dull: _____________
Mundane: _____________	Extraordinary: _____________
Nostalgic: _____________	Forward-looking: _____________
Opulent: _____________	Spartan: _____________
Placid: _____________	Turbulent: _____________
Querulous: _____________	Content: _____________
Resolute: _____________	Vacillating: _____________
Sagacious: _____________	Foolish: _____________
Tangible: _____________	Ethereal: _____________
Unruffled: _____________	Perturbed: _____________
Venerable: _____________	Disrespected: _____________
Whimsical: _____________	Serious: _____________
Yearning: _____________	Indifferent: _____________

Synonyms

Find a synonym for each word in the list below and write it on the provided line.

Warm: _____________	Cool: _____________
Wet: _____________	Dry: _____________
Fresh: _____________	Stale: _____________
Open: _____________	Shut: _____________
Sharp: _____________	Dull: _____________
Rich: _____________	Poor: _____________
Young: _____________	Old: _____________
Light: _____________	Dark: _____________
Calm: _____________	Angry: _____________
Kind: _____________	Mean: _____________
Full: _____________	Empty: _____________
Strong: _____________	Weak: _____________
Tall: _____________	Short: _____________
Fast: _____________	Slow: _____________
Smart: _____________	Dumb: _____________
Hard: _____________	Soft: _____________
Sweet: _____________	Bitter: _____________
Loud: _____________	Quiet: _____________
Neat: _____________	Messy: _____________
Clean: _____________	Dirty: _____________
Brave: _____________	Scared: _____________
Near: _____________	Far: _____________
Early: _____________	Late: _____________
Good: _____________	Bad: _____________

Synonyms

Find a synonym for each word in the list below and write it on the provided line.

Clear: _________________________	Cloudy: _________________________
Gentle: _________________________	Harsh: _________________________
Happy: _________________________	Sad: _________________________
Simple: _________________________	Complex _________________________
Brisk: _________________________	Leisurely: _________________________
Sparse: _________________________	Crowded: _________________________
Bliss: _________________________	Misery: _________________________
Crisp: _________________________	Soggy: _________________________
Sunny: _________________________	Rainy: _________________________
Chilly: _________________________	Toasty: _________________________
Lively: _________________________	Dull: _________________________
Silent: _________________________	Noisy: _________________________
Smooth: _________________________	Jagged: _________________________
Bright: _________________________	Gloomy: _________________________
Plenty: _________________________	Scarce: _________________________
Bustling: _________________________	Quiet: _________________________
Cozy: _________________________	Spacious: _________________________
Polite: _________________________	Rude: _________________________
Humble: _________________________	Proud: _________________________
Joyous: _________________________	Solemn: _________________________
Modern: _________________________	Antique: _________________________
Rapid: _________________________	Sluggish: _________________________
Tender: _________________________	Tough: _________________________
Vivid: _________________________	Pale: _________________________

Synonyms

Find a synonym for each word in the list below and write it on the provided line.

Affable:	Aloof:
Brisk:	Sluggish:
Cordial:	Unfriendly:
Dapper:	Slovenly:
Elated:	Depressed:
Frugal:	Wasteful:
Genteel:	Uncouth:
Heated:	Icy:
Idyllic:	Flawed:
Jocular:	Morose:
Knack:	Ineptitude:
Lax:	Stringent:
Mirth:	Sorrow:
Novice:	Expert:
Oblong:	Square:
Pallid:	Ruddy:
Quaint:	Mundane:
Rustic:	Polished:
Staunch:	Unreliable:
Tranquil:	Agitated:
Upbeat:	Somber:
Volatile:	Stable:
Wizened:	Youthful:
Zenith:	Nadir:

SYNONYMS

Exercise: Synonym Circle

Objective: To identify words with similar meanings by circling the correct synonym from a list of options.

How This Exercise Helps: This activity is designed to help individuals with aphasia recognize words with similar meanings, improving their vocabulary and language recognition skills.

Instructions:

1. You will find a list of words in the left column.
2. Next to each word are four choices.
3. Circle the word that is a synonym of the word in the left column.

Example:

Word   **Choices**
Happy: Sad   Angry   Pleased   Sleepy

Tips: Take your time to think about each word and its possible synonyms. If you are not sure about an answer, try to use the word in a sentence to see which synonym fits best. It's okay to skip a word and come back to it later. Don't be afraid to ask for help or use resources like a thesaurus if you are stuck.

Synonyms

In each column, circle the word that is a synonym of the given word.

Word:	Choices			
Gentle:	Harsh	Mild	Abrasive	Tough
Loud:	Silent	Noisy	Quiet	Muffled
Ancient:	Modern	Old	New	Recent
Brave:	Cowardly	Fearless	Timid	Shy
Clear:	Opaque	Transparent	Foggy	Murky
Deep:	Shallow	Profound	High	Surface
Kind:	Cruel	Generous	Mean	Harsh
Narrow:	Wide	Slim	Broad	Thick
Quick:	Speedy	Slow	Snappy	Sluggish
Rare:	Common	Unique	Usual	Ordinary
Sour:	Bitter	Tart	Sweet	Salty
Vast:	Small	Huge	Tiny	Limited
Wise:	Foolish	Smart	Ignorant	Knowledgeable
Young:	Old	Juvenile	Elderly	Mature
Zesty:	Tasteless	Spicy	Bland	Flavorless
Able:	Unable	Capable	Inept	Incompetent
Bold:	Timid	Daring	Shy	Reserved
Crisp:	Soggy	Brittle	Soft	Limp
Dense:	Sparse	Thick	Empty	Light
Eager:	Apathetic	Keen	Reluctant	Unwilling
Faint:	Bright	Dim	Loud	Clear
Grand:	Simple	Petty	Magnificent	Insignificant
Humble:	Proud	Modest	Arrogant	Boastful

Synonyms

In each column, circle the word that is a synonym of the given word.

Word:	Choices			
Breezy:	Windy	Stuffy	Calm	Hot
Chilly:	Cool	Hot	Warm	Frosty
Daring:	Bold	Cowardly	Fearful	Timid
Elegant:	Graceful	Clumsy	Rough	Plain
Fragile:	Breakable	Sturdy	Tough	Durable
Gloomy:	Sunny	Bright	Cheerful	Morose
Hearty:	Robust	Weak	Frail	Sickly
Inventive:	Uncreative	Imaginative	Dull	Routine
Jovial:	Merry	Gloomy	Sad	Morbid
Knotty:	Simple	Smooth	Straight	Tangled
Luminous:	Bright	Dark	Dull	Dim
Merry:	Joyful	Sad	Depressed	Sorrowful
Nimble:	Clumsy	Agile	Slow	Stiff
Optimistic:	Pessimistic	Hopeful	Despairing	Negative
Plentiful:	Scarce	Abundant	Lacking	Insufficient
Quaint:	Ordinary	Charming	Modern	Typical
Rustic:	Urban	Rural	Polished	Modern
Serene:	Peaceful	Agitated	Stormy	Tense
Tranquil:	Agitated	Calm	Boisterous	Upset
Ubiquitous:	Scarce	Omnipresent	Rare	Unusual
Vibrant:	Dull	Lively	Tedious	Boring
Wholesome:	Unhealthy	Nourishing	Harmful	Toxic
Youthful:	Aged	Vibrant	Old	Decrepit

Synonyms

In each column, circle the word that is a synonym of the given word.

Word:	Choices			
Brief:	Short	Long	Extended	Tall
Crafty:	Clever	Dull	Unskilled	Naive
Dull:	Sharp	Boring	Interesting	Keen
Fluent:	Stammering	Eloquent	Hesitant	Choppy
Grim:	Bright	Bleak	Cheerful	Shiny
Hefty:	Slight	Weighty	Light	Tiny
Intact:	Broken	Whole	Shattered	Divided
Jolly:	Sad	Merry	Mournful	Dismal
Kindly:	Mean	Warm	Cruel	Harsh
Lean:	Fat	Thin	Plump	Thick
Mild:	Harsh	Gentle	Bitter	Sour
Nifty:	Clumsy	Stylish	Awkward	Dated
Orderly:	Messy	Neat	Chaotic	Jumbled
Proud:	Humble	Haughty	Ashamed	Modest
Quiet:	Noisy	Hushed	Loud	Roaring
Ripe:	Green	Mature	Raw	Unripe
Sleek:	Rough	Smooth	Coarse	Bumpy
Tame:	Wild	Docile	Fierce	Savage
Unique:	Common	Singular	Normal	Usual
Vivid:	Dull	Bright	Colorless	Pale
Wary:	Careless	Cautious	Negligent	Rash
Zesty:	Flavorful	Flat	Insipid	Bland

Synonyms

In each column, circle the word that is a synonym of the given word.

Word:	Choices			
Brisk:	Quick	Slow	Lazy	Relaxed
Crisp:	Soggy	Sharp	Moist	Damp
Dense:	Sparse	Thick	Light	Airy
Eager:	Keen	Unwilling	Reluctant	Indifferent
Faint:	Clear	Dim	Bright	Loud
Glum:	Joyful	Sad	Happy	Elated
Hasty:	Slow	Rapid	Leisurely	Sluggish
Idle:	Busy	Lazy	Active	Engaged
Just:	Biased	Fair	Unequal	Partial
Lively:	Dull	Active	Sleepy	Sluggish
Meek:	Bold	Timid	Brave	Confident
Noble:	Lowly	Honorable	Ignoble	Mean
Placid:	Turbulent	Calm	Agitated	Rough
Rare:	Common	Scarce	Abundant	Frequent
Sparse:	Crowded	Thin	Packed	Abundant
Taut:	Loose	Tight	Slack	Flexible
Vast:	Tiny	Huge	Small	Narrow
Weary:	Fresh	Tired	Energetic	Alert
Adept:	Clumsy	Skilled	Inept	Awkward
Bland:	Spicy	Dull	Flavorful	Tangy
Chic:	Drab	Stylish	Outdated	Frumpy
Dapper:	Sloppy	Neat	Disheveled	Messy
Exact:	Approximate	Precise	Inexact	Vague

Synonyms

In each column, circle the word that is a synonym of the given word.

Word:	Choices			
Able:	Capable	Weak	Inept	Feeble
Blunt:	Sharp	Dull	Pointed	Keen
Cozy:	Comfy	Harsh	Unfriendly	Cold
Deft:	Clumsy	Adept	Inept	Awkward
Fair:	Unjust	Just	Biased	Crooked
Gentle:	Rough	Kind	Harsh	Brutal
Humble:	Proud	Modest	Boastful	Arrogant
Lush:	Sparse	Luxuriant	Scarce	Barren
Merry:	Sad	Joyous	Gloomy	Morose
Nimble:	Clumsy	Quick	Slow	Stiff
Pithy:	Long	Concise	Wordy	Verbose
Quaint:	Common	Charming	Usual	Standard
Rustic:	Urban	Country	Modern	Sleek
Stout:	Thin	Burly	Slender	Lean
Trim:	Messy	Neat	Cluttered	Ragged
Vocal:	Silent	Outspoken	Quiet	Mute
Witty:	Dull	Clever	Boring	Stupid
Alert:	Drowsy	Watchful	Asleep	Unaware
Breezy:	Windy	Calm	Still	Stuffy
Chill:	Warm	Cool	Hot	Toasty
Dainty:	Clumsy	Delicate	Awkward	Rough
Earthy:	Airy	Natural	Synthetic	Unnatural
Fresh:	Stale	New	Spoiled	Rotten

ANTONYMS

How This Helps

Language Rehabilitation: Antonym activities provide opportunities to practice word retrieval and expand vocabulary, addressing language challenges often faced after a stroke.

Communication Enhancement: Working with antonyms improves the ability to express ideas effectively, facilitating better communication with others.

Cognitive Stimulation: Identifying and using antonyms engages cognitive processes, such as memory and language skills, contributing to overall cognitive rehabilitation.

Confidence Building: Successfully completing antonym exercises can boost confidence, motivating stroke survivors in their recovery journey and encouraging active participation in conversations.

In summary, antonyms exercises offer a structured and beneficial way for stroke survivors to work on vocabulary, word retrieval, cognitive abilities, and communication skills. These exercises play a valuable role in language rehabilitation, helping individuals regain language fluency and confidence.

Instructions for the Antonym Activity

Understanding Antonyms: Antonyms are words that have opposite meanings. For example, "happy" and "sad" are antonyms because they have opposite meanings.

Read the Word: Start by reading the word provided. For example, if the word is "happy," your task is to create a sentence using an antonym for "happy."

Create a Sentence: Write a sentence using an antonym for the given word in the space provided. For example, for "happy," you can write "I am sad."

Antonyms

Use an antonym for the given word to create a sentence. Write the sentence in the space provided.

Nervous: ____

Interesting: ____

Dark: ____

Warm: ____

Same: ____

Inactive: ____

Forward: ____

True: ____

Bumpy: ____

Healthy: ____

Lanky: ____

Typical: ____

Liquid: ____

Complex: ____

Humble: ____

Cowardly: ____

Spicy: ____

Bald: ____

Elderly: ____

Fill: ____

Antonyms

Use an antonym for the given word to create a sentence. Write the sentence in the space provided.

Exciting: ____

Bright: ____

Empty: ____

Cool: ____

Different: ______________________________________

Active: ____

Backward: _______________________________________

False: ____

Smooth: ____

Unhealthy: ______________________________________

Short: ____

Unusual: ____

Solid: ____

Simple: ____

Arrogant: _______________________________________

Brave: ____

Mild: ____

Hairy: ____

Young: ____

Empty: ____

Antonyms

Use an antonym for the given word to create a sentence. Write the sentence in the space provided.

Wild: ____

Quiet: ____

Thin: ____

Happy: ____

Short: ____

Old: ____

Strong: ____

Light: ____

Full: ____

Simple: ____

Fast: ____

Bright: ____

Big: ____

Soft: ____

Empty: ____

Kind: ____

Young: ____

Smooth: ____

Brave: ____

Patient: ____

Antonyms

Use an antonym for the given word to create a sentence. Write the sentence in the space provided.

Cold: ____

Bright: ____

Small: ____

Happy: ____

Slow: ____

Old: ____

Calm: ____

Empty: ____

Brave: ____

Hard: ____

Full: ____

Quiet: ____

Fast: ____

Light: ____

Simple: ____

Kind: ____

Young: ____

Heavy: ____

Thin: ____

Patient: ____

Antonyms

Use an antonym for the given word to create a sentence. Write the sentence in the space provided.

Fast: ____

Light: _______________________________________

Hard: ____

Empty: _______________________________________

Young: _______________________________________

Calm: ____

Small: _______________________________________

Happy: _______________________________________

Dark: ____

Brave: _______________________________________

Thin: ____

Slow: ____

Heavy: _______________________________________

Bright: ______________________________________

Old: ____

Quiet: _______________________________________

Kind: ____

Tall: ____

Simple: ______________________________________

Full: ____

HOMONYMS

Homonym Fill-In Activity

Objective: To enhance word recognition and vocabulary by correctly identifying and using homonyms—words that sound alike but have different meanings and sometimes different spellings.

How This Exercise Helps: This exercise promotes attention to word meaning and context, which is essential for effective communication. It also aids in the distinction between words that sound similar, improving both spoken and written language skills.

Instructions:
1. **Review the Homonyms:** Familiarize yourself with the pairs of homonyms that will be used in this activity

2. **Read the Sentences:** Carefully read each sentence. Note the context clues that indicate which word meaning is required.

3. **Choose the Correct Homonym:** Determine which homonym correctly completes each sentence based on the context.

4. **Fill in the Blanks:** Write the appropriate homonym in each blank space.

Example:
Pair/pear   She enjoyed a juicy pear for breakfast and wore a comfortable pair of shoes.

Tip: Think about the meaning of each sentence as a whole before deciding which homonym to use. Say the sentence out loud with each homonym option to help determine which sounds correct. If you get stuck, consider the spelling of the homonym and if it gives a clue about its meaning   Practice makes perfect—repeat the exercise with new sentences to become more confident in using homonyms.

Homonyms

Choose the correct homonym for each blank space in the sentences provided.

1) Role/roll: She played the lead __________ in the play and wanted to eat a cinnamon __________ for dessert.

2) Scent/cent: The __________ of roses filled the air as she picked up a shiny __________ from the sidewalk.

3) Principal/principle: The school __________ upheld the __________ of fairness and honesty.

4) Sail/sale: They decided to __________ to a nearby island during the boat __________ .

5) Flour/flower: She used __________ to bake a cake and placed a fresh __________ in a vase on the table.

6) Allowed/aloud: He was __________ to sit anywhere he liked, so he read his book __________ .

7) Berry/bury: She found a ripe strawberry and decided to __________ it in the garden.

8) Break/brake: He had to __________ the car suddenly when he saw the red __________ light.

9) Peace/piece: The treaty brought __________ to the region, and they celebrated with a __________ of cake.

10) Mail/male: The __________ delivery arrived just in time, and it was addressed to a __________ recipient.

11) Mail/male: She checked the __________ for any letters and noticed a __________ cardinal perching on the mailbox.

Homonyms

Choose the correct homonym for each blank space in the sentences provided.

1) One/won: She was the ___________ who ___________ the game with her incredible skills.

2) Their/there: ___________ car was parked over ___________ by the park.

3) Weather/whether: He wondered about the ___________ forecast and ___________

   or not to bring an umbrella.

4) Passed/past: She ___________ the test with flying colors, and her success was a

   result of hard work in the ___________ .

5) Knew/new: She ___________ about the ___________ job opening and immediately applied.

6) Peace/piece: The broken vase was beyond repair, so they had to throw it away, but

   it was a beautiful ___________ .

7) Morning/mourning: The ___________ sun rose as they gathered for ___________

   at the funeral.

8) Flour/flower: The baker needed more ___________ to make bread, but stopped to smell

   the beautiful ___________ in the vase.

9) Pair/pear: She enjoyed a juicy ___________ for breakfast and wore a comfortable

   ___________ of shoes.

10) Peace/piece: The puzzle was missing one crucial ___________ that prevented it

   from being completed, causing frustration and a lack of ___________ .

11) Night/knight: The stars were bright last ___________ , and the story of the

   brave ___________ always lulled her to sleep.

Homonyms

Choose the correct homonym for each blank space in the sentences provided.

1) Pair/pear: She enjoyed a juicy ___________ for breakfast and   wore a comfortable ___________ of shoes.

2) Peace/piece: The broken vase was beyond repair, so they had to throw it away, but it was a beautiful ___________ .

3) Morning/mourning: The ___________ sun rose as they gathered for ___________ at the funeral.

4) Aisle/isle: She walked down the ___________ of the grocery store to find her favorite snacks.

5) Knew/new: She ___________ about the ___________ job opening and immediately applied.

6) Peace/piece: The puzzle was missing one crucial ___________ that prevented it from being completed, causing frustration and a lack of ___________ .

7) Weather/whether: He wondered about the ___________ forecast and ___________ or not to bring an umbrella.

8) Passed/past: She ___________ the test with flying colors, and her success was a result of hard work in the ___________ .

9) Their/there: ___________ car was parked over ___________ by the park.

10) Knew/new: She ___________ gabout the ___________ job opening and immediately applied.

11) Sea/see: The sailor looked out at the vast ___________ , hoping to ___________ land soon.

Homonyms

Choose the correct homonym for each blank space in the sentences provided.

1) Peace/piece: The __________ in the neighborhood was evident as neighbors shared

   a __________ of cake.

2) Break/brake: Remember to __________ gently when approaching a red __________ light.

3) Morning/mourning: The __________ dew glistened in the __________ sun as they

   paid their respects.

4) Principal/principle: The __________ of the school ensured that the __________

   of fairness was upheld.

5) One/won: She was the __________ who __________ the game with her incredible skills.

6) Allowed/aloud: He was __________ to sit anywhere he liked, so he read his

   book __________ .

7) Berry/bury: She found a ripe strawberry and decided to __________ it in the garden.

8) Weather/whether: He wondered about the __________ forecast and __________

   or not to bring an umbrella.

9) Passed/past: She __________ the test with flying colors, and her success was a result

   of hard work in the __________ .

10) Knew/new: She __________ about the __________ job opening and immediately applied.

11) Son/sun: The __________ came up early, which woke up her young __________

    for his first day of school.

12) Bare/bear: The tree was __________ of leaves, and in the distance,

    a large __________ roamed the forest.

Homonyms

Choose the correct homonym for each blank space in the sentences provided.

1) Role/roll: She played the lead __________ in the play and wanted to eat a cinnamon __________ for dessert.

2) Scent/cent: The __________ of roses filled the air as she picked up a shiny __________ from the sidewalk.

3) Sail/sale: They decided to __________ to a nearby island during the boat __________ .

4) Blue/blew: The sky was a clear __________ , and the wind __________ the fallen leaves across the yard.

5) Simple/symple: The __________ design of the logo conveyed a __________ message to customers.

6) New/knew: She __________ about the __________ job opening and immediately applied.

7) Morning/mourning: The __________ sun rose as they gathered for __________ at the funeral.

8) Peace/piece: The puzzle was missing one crucial __________ that prevented it from being completed, causing frustration and a lack of __________ .

9) Their/there: __________ car was parked over __________ by the park.

10) Role/roll: She played the __________ of a baker and needed to __________ out the dough for the bread.

11) Hole/whole: He dug a __________ in the backyard to plant a tree, aiming to eat its fruit the __________ summer.

COLLECTIVE NOUNS

Collective Noun Activity Instructions

Objective:
To improve understanding and usage of collective nouns, which are specific words that denote groups of people, animals, or things.

How This Exercise Helps:
This activity enhances language skills by familiarizing you with collective nouns, encouraging you to recognize and correctly associate them with their corresponding groups. It's particularly beneficial for those working to improve language recall and categorization skills.

Instructions:
Read the Columns: You'll find two columns. Column 1 contains a list of collective nouns (e.g., "herd"), while Column 2 lists various animals or objects (e.g., "cattle").

Match the Pairs: Your task is to match each collective noun in Column 1 with its appropriate animal or object in Column 2. For instance, "herd" should be matched with "cattle."

Record Your Matches: Once you've identified a match, either write the matched pairs in the provided space, or visually indicate the matches. This could be done by drawing a line between the collective noun and its corresponding animal/object, or writing the collective noun next to the relevant item.

Tips: Take your time to think about each pair. If you're unsure, move on and come back to it later. Some collective nouns can be used for multiple groups, so focus on the most common or well-known associations. Feel free to use additional resources or ask for help if you're stuck on a particular pair.

Collective nouns

Draw a line to match the collective noun on the left with its correct group on the right.

1. Flock of	lions
2. School of	geese
3. Herd of	kittens
4. Pack of	dolphins
5. Swarm of	monkeys
6. Troop of	cattle
7. Colony of	flowers
8. Pride of	fish
9. Pod of	horses
10. Gaggle of	bees
11. Team of	kangaroos
12. Parliament of	grapes
13. Litter of	actors
14. Mob of	wolves
15. Bunch of	ships
16. Staff of	employees
17. Bouquet of	ants
18. Band of	musicians
19. Fleet of	owls
20. Troupe of	kittens

Collective Nouns

Draw a line to match the collective noun on the left with its correct group on the right.

1. Murder of		sticks
2. Fleet of		penguins
3. Swarm of		singers
4. School of		stairs
5. Parliament of		bats
6. Troop of		crows
7. Litter of		dolphins
8. Choir of		athletes
9. Pack of		ants
10. Flight of		spectators
11. Gang of		cards
12. Team of		locusts
13. Orchestra of		hikers
14. Cloud of		thieves
15. Crash of		musicians
16. Army of		owls
17. Bundle of		rhinos
18. Colony of		puppies
19. Audience of		cars
20. Band of		scouts

Collective Nouns

Draw a line to match the collective noun on the left with its correct group on the right.

1. Batch of	seagulls
2. Brood of	toads
3. Bale of	roses
4. Clutch of	leaves
5. Swarm of	witches
6. Bevy of	researchers
7. Bundle of	soldiers
8. Flight of	bikers
9. Bouquet of	chicks
10. Crew of	airplanes
11. Coven of	hay
12. Suite of	whales
13. Fleet of	cookies
14. Gang of	actors
15. Team of	joy
16. Cast of	sailors
17. Knot of	eggs
18. School of	soldiers
19. Pile of	rooms
20. Army of	butterflies

Collective Nouns

Draw a line to match the collective noun on the left with its correct group on the right.

1. Fleet of	butterflies
2. School of	researchers
3. Swarm of	seagulls
4. Bevy of	toads
5. Bouquet of	leaves
6. Clutch of	witches
7. Crew of	roses
8. Army of	bikers
9. Gang of	chicks
10. Flight of	airplanes
11. Batch of	hay
12. Cast of	whales
13. Knot of	cookies
14. Brood of	actors
15. Suite of	joy
16. Pile of	sailors
17. Team of	eggs
18. Bundle of	soldiers
19. Coven of	rooms
20. Bunch of	joy

Collective Nouns

Draw a line to match the collective noun on the left with its correct group on the right.

1. Troop of	lions
2. Gaggle of	geese
3. Pack of	cards
4. Choir of	singers
5. Quiver of	arrows
6. Murder of	crows
7. Parliament of	owls
8. Pride of	lions
9. Pod of	dolphins
10. Stack of	books
11. Troupe of	dancers
12. Colony of	penguins
13. Flock of	birds
14. Herd of	elephants
15. Litter of	puppies
16. Nest of	vipers
17. Band of	musicians
18. Array of	stars
19. Glaring of	cats
20. Regiment of	soldiers

PHRASE COMPLETION

Phrase Completion Activity Instructions

Objective:
Build language skills by completing common phrases.

How This Exercise Helps:
This activity aids in reinforcing common phrase structures and vocabulary, which can be particularly beneficial for individuals with aphasia working on sentence construction and word retrieval.

Instructions:
Review Phrases: Look at the phrases with blanks.
Complete Phrases: Add words that make sense contextually.
Check Answers: Ensure completed phrases are logical.
Try Alternates: Think of different words that could also fit.

Tips: Use everyday words and actions for completion. More than one answer may be correct. If unsure, think about what words you'd use in a conversation.

Examples:
Mow the ___________ (e.g., "lawn").
Wash the ___________ (e.g., "dishes").

Complete the phrases with appropriate words. Focus on common and practical uses.

Phrase Completion

Complete each phrase by filling in the blank with a suitable word or words that complete the phrase. There may be more than one correct answer for each phrase.

1. Pretty as a _______________
2. You won a _______________
3. Running out of _______________
4. Cool as a _______________
5. Grab a cup of _______________
6. From start to _______________
7. Mow the _______________
8. Happy as a _______________
9. Wash the _______________
10. Have a nice _______________
11. Caught in a traffic _______________
12. On the tip of my _______________
13. From one end to the _______________
14. Thunder and _______________
15. Mad as a _______________
16. Take it or _______________
17. My pride and _______________
18. Won fair and _______________
19. Fought tooth and _______________
20. In sickness and in _______________
21. On top of the _______________
22. A piece of _______________
23. A slice of _______________
24. Like two peas in a _______________
25. The early bird catches the _______________

Phrase Completion

Complete each phrase by filling in the blank with a suitable word or words that complete the phrase. There may be more than one correct answer for each phrase.

1. A penny for your ______________
2. Actions speak louder than ______________
3. A watched pot never ______________
4. Don't count your chickens before they ______________
5. Don't put all your eggs in one ______________
6. Don't throw the baby out with the ______________
7. Every cloud has a silver ______________
8. Give him an inch, and he'll take a ______________
9. Haste makes ______________
10. If the shoe fits, ______________
11. It takes two to ______________
12. Let the cat out of the ______________
13. Many hands make light ______________
14. Out of sight, out of ______________
15. People who live in glass houses shouldn't throw ______________
16. Rome wasn't built in a ______________
17. The apple doesn't fall far from the ______________
18. The early bird gets the ______________
19. The grass is always greener on the other ______________
20. The pen is mightier than the ______________
21. The pot calling the kettle ______________
22. There's no smoke without ______________
23. Two heads are better than ______________
24. When in Rome, do as the ______________
25. You can't make an omelette without breaking ______________

Phrase Completion

Complete each phrase by filling in the blank with a suitable word or words that complete the phrase. There may be more than one correct answer for each phrase.

1. A picture is worth a thousand __________
2. Actions speak louder than __________
3. A watched kettle never __________
4. All that glitters is not __________
5. An apple a day keeps the __________
6. Barking up the wrong __________
7. Beauty is in the eye of the __________
8. Birds of a feather flock __________
9. Curiosity killed the __________
10. Don't cry over spilled __________
11. Don't put all your eggs in one __________
12. Easy come, easy __________
13. Every cloud has a silver __________
14. Fool me once, shame on __________
15. Give a man a hammer, and he'll build a __________
16. Haste makes __________
17. If the shoe fits, __________
18. It's a piece of __________
19. Let the cat out of the __________
20. Money doesn't grow on __________
21. People who live in glass houses shouldn't throw __________
22. Rome wasn't built in a __________
23. The early bird gets the __________
24. The grass is always greener on the other __________
25. When in Rome, do as the __________

Phrase Completion

Complete each phrase by filling in the blank with a suitable word or words that complete the phrase. There may be more than one correct answer for each phrase.

1. A needle in a ___________
2. As cool as a ___________
3. A penny saved is a penny ___________
4. Bee in your ___________
5. Clean as a ___________
6. Don't bite the hand that ___________
7. Down the ___________
8. Face the ___________
9. Home is where the ___________
10. In the blink of an ___________
11. Life is a ___________
12. Like father, like ___________
13. Night and ___________
14. Off the ___________
15. On the ___________
16. Over the ___________
17. Penny for your ___________
18. Put your best ___________
19. Right up my ___________
20. Silver ___________
21. Still waters run ___________
22. Straight from the ___________
23. Take the bull by the ___________
24. The calm before the ___________
25. Two heads are better than ___________

Phrase Completion

Complete each phrase by filling in the blank with a suitable word or words that complete the phrase. There may be more than one correct answer for each phrase.

1. A stitch in time saves __________
2. All is fair in love and __________
3. Beauty is only __________
4. Catch someone red-__________
5. Cut to the __________
6. Don't count your chickens before they __________
7. Don't throw the baby out with the __________
8. Every dog has its __________
9. Fight fire with __________
10. Fish out of __________
11. Get out of the wrong side of the __________
12. Good things come to those who __________
13. Hit the nail on the __________
14. If the shoe fits, __________
15. Let the cat out of the __________
16. Money is the root of all __________
17. Once bitten, twice __________
18. Put your best __________
19. Right up my __________
20. Sink or __________
21. Spill the __________
22. Take it or __________
23. Two heads are better __________
24. When in Rome, do as the __________
25. You can lead a horse to water, but you can't make it __________

SENTENCE COMPLETION
Sentence Completion Activity Instructions

Objective:
To practice selecting the appropriate word to complete a sentence accurately.

How This Exercise Helps:
Improves decision-making in word selection and strengthens sentence structure understanding.

Instructions:
Examine the Sentence: Begin with the sentence provided, such as "Before bed, I always ________________."

Choose Wisely: Pick a suitable word from the options given (e.g., read, eat, dance).

Fill in the Gap: Insert the selected word into the blank to complete the thought.

Verify Your Choice: Confirm that the completed sentence is coherent and contextually appropriate.

Tip: Focus on the sentence's overall meaning to guide your choice. Remember, there can be multiple correct answers; "Before bed, I always read" is just as valid as "Before bed, I always brush my teeth." If multiple options seem correct, choose the one that is most likely in a typical scenario.

Sentence Completion

Choose the word from the options in parentheses that best completes each sentence. Write your choice in the blank provided.

1. She wore a beautiful ____________. (hat, cat, car)
2. I enjoy eating fresh ____________. (pears, cars, stars)
3. The children built a sandcastle at the ____________. (beach, bench, branch)
4. He likes to play the guitar and sing ____________. (songs, socks, snakes)
5. The sky was filled with fluffy white ____________. (clouds, cows, coats)
6. She drank a glass of cold ____________. (water, winter, waiter)
7. The puppy chased its tail in a circle, looking _________.(happy, hippo, hot)
8. The teacher wrote the lesson on the ____________. (board, bird, bread)
9. I took a long walk through the ____________. (forest, fork, fountain)
10. He read a fascinating ____________. (book, boot, bat)
11. We had a picnic in the ____________. (park, dark, shark)
12. The sun set behind the ____________. (mountain, fountain, curtain)
13. The magician pulled a rabbit out of his ____________. (hat, cat, bat)
14. The baby smiled at the ____________. (moon, spoon, balloon)
15. The chef cooked a delicious ____________. (meal, seal, wheel)
16. The children played in the ____________. (yard, card, lard)
17. The dog chased the ____________. (ball, call, wall)
18. I found a shiny ____________. (coin, loin, join)
19. The fire crackled in the ____________. (fireplace, staircase, suitcase)
20. She received a red ____________. (rose, hose, nose)
21. The airplane flew high in the ____________. (sky, fly, pie)
22. The baby took its first ____________. (step, steep, sleep)
23. The fish swam in the clear ____________. (water, waiter, wander)
24. The hiker climbed a steep ____________. (hill, grill, pill)
25. He played a tune on his ____________. (guitar, car, star)

Sentence Completion

Choose the word from the options in parentheses that best completes each sentence.
Write your choice in the blank provided.

1. I found a shiny ___________ in the sand. (shell, smell, sell)
2. The ___________ was covered in snow. (mountain, fountain, maintain)
3. She wore a ___________ dress to the party. (sparkly, spiky, spooky)
4. He put on his ___________ and tie for the interview. (suit, sweet, suit)
5. The children played tag in the ___________. (garden, guardian, garland)
6. I heard a loud ___________ from the car engine. (noise, nose, noodles)
7. The cat chased a ___________ across the yard. (squirrel, square, squeeze)
8. The ___________ was full of interesting exhibits. (museum, muesli, muscle)
9. She gave her friend a ___________ for their birthday. (gift, grift, graft)
10. I need to ___________ my bicycle tire. (inflate, inflate, inflow)
11. The ___________ barked at the mailman. (dog, log, fog)
12. I love the taste of freshly baked ___________. (bread, breed, bead)
13. He fixed the broken ___________ with a hammer. (fence, fence, fester)
14. We took a walk in the ___________. (park, parka, peak)
15. She received a beautiful ___________. (ring, sing, sling)
16. The ___________ sang a melodious song. (bird, beard, board)
17. She wore a bright ___________ to the beach. (bikini, biker, biplane)
18. The ___________ was shining brightly. (sun, son, bun)
19. He was covered in mud from head to ___________. (toe, tow, too)
20. The ___________ flew through the sky. (plane, plan, plank)
21. The ___________ sailed across the ocean. (ship, sheep, sharp)
22. I saw a beautiful ___________ in the garden. (flower, flour, floor)
23. He carved a pumpkin for ___________. (Halloween, hall, hail)
24. The ___________ was full of tasty treats. (bakery, battery, bitter)
25. She wore a ___________ hat to the beach. (straw, straw, strum)

Sentence Completion

Choose the word from the options in parentheses that best completes each sentence.
Write your choice in the blank provided.

1. The flowers in the garden bloom in ____________. (spring, swing, sing)

2. He lost his ____________ in the forest. (way, weigh, whey)

3. I need to buy some fresh ____________. (bread, thread, dread)

4. The children played with colorful ____________. (kites, bites, rights)

5. She picked up the ____________ and answered it. (phone, cone, bone)

6. The baby took its first ____________. (step, steep, sleep)

7. He opened the ____________ to let in fresh air. (window, widow, wind)

8. The ____________ jumped over the fence. (rabbit, habit, cabinet)

9. The ____________ cooked a delicious meal. (chef, chief, thief)

10. We enjoyed a ____________ of ice cream on a hot day. (cone, bone, phone)

11. The cat curled up on the ____________. (sofa, sofa, sofa)

12. He fixed the broken ____________. (bike, bake, beak)

13. The teacher praised her for her hard ____________. (work, fork, cork)

14. We celebrated with a birthday ____________. (cake, rake, lake)

15. I always brush my ____________ before bed. (teeth, teeth, teeth)

16. The bird sang a sweet ____________. (song, gong, long)

17. She wears a beautiful ____________. (dress, dress, dress)

18. The rain began to ____________. (fall, fall, fall)

19. He painted the ____________ with bright colors. (canvas, canvas, canvas)

20. The children played with colorful ____________. (blocks, socks, rocks)

21. I'm going to visit my ____________ in the hospital. (grandma, grandpa, panda)

22. The ____________ is rising in the east. (sun, bun, run)

23. The cat chased the ____________ up a tree. (squirrel, bat, car)

24. The ____________ made a funny noise. (car, jar, far)

25. The ____________ sang a lullaby. (mother, brother, smother)

Sentence Completion

Choose the word from the options in parentheses that best completes each sentence. Write your choice in the blank provided.

1. The flowers in the garden bloom in ____________. (spring, swing, sing)
2. He lost his ____________ in the forest. (way, weigh, whey)
3. I need to buy some fresh ____________. (bread, thread, dread)
4. The children played with colorful ____________. (kites, bites, rights)
5. She picked up the ____________ and answered it. (phone, cone, bone)
6. The baby took its first ____________. (step, steep, sleep)
7. He opened the ____________ to let in fresh air. (window, widow, wind)
8. The ____________ jumped over the fence. (rabbit, habit, cabinet)
9. The ____________ cooked a delicious meal. (chef, chief, thief)
10. We enjoyed a ____________ of ice cream on a hot day. (cone, bone, phone)
11. The cat curled up on the ____________. (sign, sofa, water)
12. He fixed the broken ____________. (bike, bake, beak)
13. The teacher praised her for her hard ____________. (work, fork, cork)
14. We celebrated with a birthday ____________. (cake, rake, lake)
15. I always brush my ____________ before bed. (teeth, feet, tooth)
16. The bird sang a sweet ____________. (song, gong, long)
17. She wears a beautiful ____________. (dress, dress, dress)
18. The rain began to ____________. (fall, fall, fall)
19. He painted the ____________ with bright colors. (water, canvas, rabbit)
20. The children played with colorful ____________. (blocks, socks, rocks)
21. I'm going to visit my __________ in the hospital. (grandma, grandpa, panda)
22. The ____________ is rising in the east. (sun, bun, run)
23. The cat chased the __________ up a tree. (squirrel, bat, car)
24. The ____________ made a funny noise. (car, jar, far)
25. The ____________ sang a lullaby. (mother, brother, smother)

Sentence Completion

Choose the word from the options in parentheses that best completes each sentence. Write your choice in the blank provided.

1. The sun sets in the ____________. (west, vest, nest)
2. The ____________ was full of colorful fish. (aquarium, auditorium, asteroid)
3. She wore a beautiful ____________. (necklace, nickname, knock)
4. He took a ____________ after a long hike. (shower, shroud, shout)
5. The children built a sandcastle at the __________.(beach, bleach, branch)
6. The puppy chased its tail in a __________. (circle, circus, cereal)
7. I like to read a ____________ before bedtime. (book, brook, broke)
8. The ____________ was shining brightly. (sun, son, bun)
9. She gave her friend a warm ____________. (hug, hog, hug)
10. I need to buy some fresh ____________. (fruit, flute, fluke)
11. The ____________ barked loudly. (dog, fog, frog)
12. I enjoy a good ____________ in the morning. (coffee, toffee, coffin)
13. He played a tune on his ____________. (guitar, cigar, radar)
14. The children played with colorful ____________. (balloons, baboons, baboons)
15. She received a beautiful ____________. (flower, flour, floor)
16. The ____________ is rising in the east. (sun, son, bun)
17. I love the smell of fresh ____________. (bread, breed, bead)
18. He fixed the broken ____________. (window, widow, wind)
19. We had a picnic in the ____________. (park, parka, peak)
20. The ____________ sang a sweet melody. (bird, beard, board)
21. She wore a pretty ____________. (dress, drill, dill)
22. The ____________ is shining through the clouds. (sun, son, bun)
23. I lost my ____________ in the forest. (way, weigh, whey)
24. He read a ____________ to the children. (story, storey, stowaway)
25. The ____________ chirped outside the window. (birds, bards, boards)

MORPHOLOGY

Morphology Exercise Instructions

Objective:
Enhance your understanding of word forms and their correct use in sentences.

How This Exercise Helps:
Develops morphological awareness, which is the recognition, understanding, and use of word parts that carry significance.

Instructions:
Start with the Sentence: Read the provided sentence. Example: "The dog ______________ loudly."

Context Analysis: Determine the necessary part of speech and tense. For this example, a verb in the past tense is needed.

Choose Correctly: Select the word that grammatically fits the sentence from the given options (e.g., bark, barked, barking). "The dog barked loudly" is the correct completion.

Tip: Consider the sentence structure and meaning to guide your choice. Pay attention to verb tenses and pluralization that might be required. There may be more than one correct morphological form, choose the one that best matches the sentence.

Morphology

Complete the sentences below with the best choice from the provided options:

1. I saw a _________ in the garden. (flower, floured, flowery)
2. She wore a _________ dress to the party. (sparkly, spiky, spooky)
3. He put on his _______ and tie for the interview. (suit, sweet, suit)
4. The children played tag in the __________. (garden, guardian, garland)
5. The cat chased a __________ across the yard. (squirrel, square, squeeze)
6. I heard a loud __________ from the car engine. (noise, nose, noodles)
7. The __________ is shining brightly. (sun, son, bun)
8. She received a beautiful __________. (ring, sing, sling)
9. The __________ sang a melodious song. (bird, beard, board)
10. She wore a bright __________ to the beach. (bikini, biker, biplane)
11. He was covered in mud from head to __________. (toe, tow, too)
12. The __________ flew through the sky. (plane, plan, plank)
13. The __________ sailed across the ocean. (ship, sheep, sharp)
14. I saw a beautiful __________ in the garden. (flower, flour, floor)
15. He carved a pumpkin for __________. (Halloween, hall, hail)
16. The __________ was full of tasty treats. (bakery, battery, bitter)
17. She wore a __________ hat to the beach. (straw, straw, strum)
18. We went on a __________ ride at the fair. (ferry, fairy, furry)
19. He has a __________ beard. (bushy, busy, bush)
20. She has a __________ voice. (lovely, lonely, lonely)
21. The __________ in the sky was beautiful. (moon, moan, mown)
22. The __________ in the zoo were playful. (monkeys, moneys, monkey's)
23. He made a __________ sculpture. (clay, clay, clei)
24. The __________ is playing hide and seek. (sun, son, bun)
25. She wore a __________ dress to the ball. (shiny, shiney, shinny)

Morphology

Complete the sentences below with the best choice from the provided options:

1. The ___________ smells wonderful. (flowers, flours, floor's)
2. He wore a ___________ suit to the wedding. (black, blacked, blacken)
3. She looked at the ___________ painting. (beautiful, beauty, beautifully)
4. The ___________ was crowded with people. (beach, bitch, beached)
5. He took a bite of the delicious ___________. (sandwich, sandal, sandy)
6. I can see the ___________ in the clear sky. (moon, moan, mown)
7. She found a ___________ in her shoe. (pebble, pebbles, pebbly)
8. The ___________ danced gracefully. (ballerina, ballerino, ballerin)
9. He won the ___________ race. (bicycle, bicycled, bicyclist)
10. The ___________ rumbled loudly. (thunder, thundery, thundered)
11. She used a ___________ to brush her hair. (comb, combats, combat)
12. The ___________ melted in the sun. (snow, snows, snowy)
13. He wore a ___________ tie to the party. (bright, brightly, brighten)
14. She planted colorful ___________ in the garden. (flowers, flows, flour)
15. The ___________ bird sang a sweet melody. (song, sing, sung)
16. He carried a heavy ___________ up the hill. (suitcase, suitable, suitcases)
17. The ___________ was delicious. (cake, caked, cakes)
18. She put a ___________ note in his lunchbox. (lovely, love, lover)
19. The ___________ shone brightly. (lighthouse, light, lights)
20. The ___________ road led to the forest. (narrow, narrowed, narrower)
21. He had a ___________ dream last night. (strange, strangely, stranger)
22. She tied a ___________ around the package. (ribbon, ribbons, ribbed)
23. The ___________ fell from the tree. (leaves, leafs, leaf)
24. He has a great sense of ___________. (humor, humorous, humors)
25. The ___________ flew gracefully over the water. (swan, swank, swarmed)

Morphology

Complete the sentences below with the best choice from the provided options:

1. The ___________ shines in the sky. (sun, son, soon)
2. She wore a beautiful ___________. (gown, gone, goon)
3. He has a ___________ personality. (friendly, friend, friends)
4. The ___________ river flows quietly. (peace, piece, peas)
5. She found a shiny ___________. (coin, coyn, coins)
6. He likes to ___________ his bicycle. (ride, rode, road)
7. The ___________ flower smells sweet. (blooming, bloom, blooms)
8. The ___________ cat purred softly. (curious, curiously, curiosity)
9. The ___________ is setting. (sun, son, soon)
10. She has a lovely ___________. (smile, smiled, smiles)
11. He painted the ___________ wall. (entire, entirely, entry)
12. The ___________ wind blew leaves. (gentle, gently, gentiles)
13. She had a ___________ dream. (wonder, wondered, wonderful)
14. He tied a ___________ on the package. (bow, bough, bowing)
15. The ___________ road leads to the beach. (sandy, sand, sands)
16. She baked a delicious ___________. (cake, caked, cakes)
17. He has a great sense of ___________. (humor, humorous, humors)
18. The ___________ bird sang a sweet melody. (song, sing, sung)
19. The ___________ book is on the shelf. (red, read, reed)
20. She placed the ___________ on the table. (plate, plated, plates)
21. The ___________ tree is tall. (pine, pined, pines)
22. He found a ___________ in the forest. (hidden, hide, hides)
23. The ___________ sky is clear. (blue, blew, bloom)
24. She enjoys a hot ___________. (chocolate, chock, choc)
25. He tied his ___________ shoes. (shoelace, shoelaces, shoeless)

Morphology

Complete the sentences below with the best choice from the provided options:

1. The ___________ bloom in spring. (flower, flow, flew)
2. He bought a new ___________. (carrot, car, care)
3. She wore a beautiful ___________. (neck, necked, necklace)
4. The ___________ of music filled the room. (sound, sounding, sounds)
5. He likes to ___________ on weekends. (relax, relaxed, relaxing)
6. The ___________ house was haunted. (old, older, oldest)
7. The ___________ apple tasted sweet. (red, redder, reddest)
8. The ___________ dog wagged its tail. (happy, happier, happiest)
9. The ___________ of rain on the roof was soothing. (sound, sounding, sounds)
10. She has a ___________ collection of stamps. (large, larger, largest)
11. He played a ___________ melody on the piano. (beautiful, beautify, beauties)
12. The ___________ tree stood tall. (oak, oaks, oaken)
13. She had a ___________ idea. (creative, creator, create)
14. He carried a heavy ___________ up the stairs. (box, boxed, boxes)
15. The ___________ river is crystal clear. (mountain, mountains, mountainous)
16. She baked delicious ___________. (cookie, cookies, cook)
17. He enjoys the ___________ of the ocean. (sound, sounding, sounds)
18. The ___________ butterfly landed on a flower. (colorful, color, coloring)
19. She found a ___________ in the attic. (treasure, treasures, treasuring)
20. He tied a ___________ on the gift. (ribbon, ribbons, ribbing)
21. The ___________ cat chased a mouse. (playful, played, plays)
22. He built a sturdy ___________. (bridge, bridges, bridging)
23. The ___________ bird sings beautifully. (song, songs, singing)
24. She read a ___________ story. (wonderful, wonders, wondered)
25. He laced up his ___________ sneakers. (athletic, athlete, athletics)

Morphology

Complete the sentences below with the best choice from the provided options:

1. The chef prepared a delicious ___________. (dine, dining, dinner)
2. She wrote a heartfelt ___________ to her friend. (letter, letters, lettering)
3. The ___________ of the mountain was breathtaking. (height, higher, highest)
4. He found an old ___________ in the attic. (book, books, booking)
5. The ___________ cat curled up on the couch. (sleep, sleeping, sleeps)
6. The ___________ of the forest was calm and serene. (silence, silent, silently)
7. He wore a bright ___________ shirt to the party. (color, colorful, coloring)
8. She had a lovely ___________ in her garden. (rose, roses, rosy)
9. The ___________ athlete won the race. (fast, faster, fastest)
10. He had a ___________ sense of humor. (great, greater, greatest)
11. She received a beautiful ___________ on her birthday. (gift, gifted, gifting)
12. The ___________ river flowed gently. (meander, meandering, meanders)
13. He displayed a stunning ___________ of artwork. (collection, collect, collecting)
14. The ___________ bird sang melodiously. (song, songs, singing)
15. The ___________ garden was full of colorful blooms. (flower, flowers, flowering)
16. She enjoyed the ___________ of a good book. (read, reading, reads)
17. The ___________ clouds drifted lazily across the sky. (white, whiten, whitest)
18. He bought a ___________ shirt for the interview. (new, newer, newest)
19. She had a ___________ idea for the project. (creative, creator, create)
20. The butterfly fluttered its ___________ wings. (colorful, colorfully, coloring)
21. He built a small ___________ for his children. (play, playing, playground)
22. She admired the ___________ view from the hilltop. (panoramic, panorama, panoramas)
23. The ___________ artist painted a beautiful landscape. (sketch, sketches, sketching)
24. He discovered a hidden ___________ in the woods. (cave, caves, caving)
25. She wrote a heartfelt ___________ to express her feelings. (message, messages, messaging)

WHAT, WHERE, WHO, WHEN, WHY, HOW

Objective:
Enhance comprehension and verbal expression by answering questions starting with What, Where, Who, When, Why, and How.

How This Exercise Helps:
This activity encourages understanding of different types of questions and promotes concise, relevant responses. It is also a practical way to practice everyday language use.

Instructions:
Read the Question: Look at each question carefully. Example: "Where do you go to buy groceries?"

Provide a Short Answer: Respond with a single word or a short phrase. For the given example, an appropriate answer would be "Supermarket."

Tips:
Focus on the question word to understand what kind of information is being asked for.
Keep your answer relevant and to the point.
Practice out loud if possible to aid in verbal fluency.

"What" Questions

Answer each question with a single word or a brief phrase that best fits the question.
You can say your answer aloud or write it on a separate piece of paper.

1. What hangs on a wall and lists days of the week and months of the year?

2. What do you call the facial hair that grows on a man's chin?

3. What is the red condiment many people put on french fries?

4. What do you use to wash your hair?

5. What is the opposite of "small"?

6. What do you call the device you use to control the television?

7. What do you use to open a door with a lock?

8. What do you call a book with blank pages for writing personal thoughts?

9. What is the frozen treat made from flavored ice and sugar?

10. What do you use to send a quick message to someone over the internet?

11. What do you call the meal you eat in the morning to break your overnight fast?

12. What is the name for a long, thin, cylindrical pasta?

13. What do you call the place where you can see a collection of art pieces?

14. What is the tool used to write on paper?

15. What do you call the device used to measure temperature?

16. What is the term for a picture taken of oneself, with a smartphone?

17. What do you call the act of making a decision between two or more options?

18. What is the opposite of "hard"?

19. What do you use to carry your books to school?

20. What is the word for a building where books are borrowed and read?

21. What is the substance that falls from the sky as rain, snow, or hail?

22. What do you call a sweet, carbonated beverage?

23. What is the term for the meal you eat in the evening?

24. What do you use to cut paper into different shapes?

25. What is the name for a person who repairs electrical appliances?

"What" Questions

Answer each question with a single word or a brief phrase that best fits the question. You can say your answer aloud or write it on a separate piece of paper.

1. What do you call the flying insect that buzzes around and can sting you?

2. What is the round, sweet fruit that comes in various colors and flavors?

3. What do you use to keep food cold in your kitchen?

4. What is the action of looking through a book or magazine quickly?

5. What is the name for a doctor who specializes in the heart?

6. What do you call the soft, cushioned piece of furniture for sitting?

7. What is the term for the number of years a person has lived?

8. What is the act of putting words and ideas onto paper or a computer screen?

9. What do you call the large, round celestial object that orbits Earth at night?

10. What is the colorful, explosive display seen in the sky on July 4th?

11. What do you use to make phone calls when you're away from home?

12. What is the green vegetable that you often find in salads?

13. What is the action of capturing images with a camera?

14. What do you call the device that shows you the time and date?

15. What is the name for the place where you buy and borrow books?

16. What do you use to protect your head from the rain or sun?

17. What is the term for the feeling of great happiness?

18. What is the opposite of "dark"?

19. What do you call the furry pet that often says "meow"?

20. What is the device you use to listen to music with headphones?

21. What is the action of looking at something closely to see details?

22. What do you call the part of your body that helps you see?

23. What is the sweet dessert made from milk and sugar, often with fruit?

24. What is the word for the act of moving through water using your limbs?

25. What do you use to write with on a piece of paper?

"What" Questions

Answer each question with a single word or a brief phrase that best fits the question.
You can say your answer aloud or write it on a separate piece of paper.

1. What is the opposite of "dark"?
2. What do you call the place where you buy groceries?
3. What is the term for a written message sent to someone far away?
4. What do you use to cut paper in a decorative way?
5. What is the device used to tell time?
6. What is the name for a round object that bounces?
7. What is the action of inhaling and exhaling to stay alive?
8. What is the word for a person who creates art using pencils or paints?
9. What do you call a piece of bread with cheese and other ingredients on top?
10. What is the term for a person who flies an aircraft?
11. What is the place where you keep your clothes?
12. What do you use to write on a piece of paper?
13. What is the word for the meal you eat in the middle of the day?
14. What do you call the large, bright object in the sky during the day?
15. What is the substance used to clean dirty dishes?
16. What is the device used to listen to music with headphones?
17. What do you call a person who studies the stars and planets?
18. What is the term for a book that tells stories about made-up characters?
19. What do you use to make a room brighter?
20. What is the action of moving through the air using wings?
21. What is the opposite of "cold"?
22. What do you call a vehicle with four wheels that you drive?
23. What is the device used to store and play video games?
24. What is the place where you take a bath or shower?
25. What is the action of making a sound by striking two objects together?

"Where" Questions

Answer each question with a single word or a brief phrase that best fits the question.
You can say your answer aloud or write it on a separate piece of paper.

1. Where do you go to see a doctor?
2. Where can you find books to read?
3. Where does a pilot fly an airplane?
4. Where is the place to buy fresh fruits and vegetables?
5. Where do you sleep at night?
6. Where can you watch a movie on a big screen?
7. Where do you find information on the internet?
8. Where is a common place to take a shower?
9. Where can you play with swings and slides?
10. Where do you go to send a letter to a friend?
11. Where can you buy tickets to travel on a train?
12. Where is a place to enjoy a sunny day near water?
13. Where do you find ingredients to cook a meal?
14. Where can you watch live performances of plays and music?
15. Where is a location to borrow books for free?
16. Where do you usually wait for a bus or train?
17. Where can you find information about history and art?
18. Where is a place to learn new things from teachers?
19. Where do you put your dirty clothes before washing them?
20. Where can you see a variety of animals from around the world?
21. Where do you go to see works of art like paintings and sculptures?
22. Where is a spot to enjoy a picnic with family and friends?
23. Where can you find fresh produce and other groceries?
24. Where do you often gather with friends for meals and drinks?
25. Where can you go to see a wide variety of plants and flowers?

"Where" Questions

Answer each question with a single word or a brief phrase that best fits the question.
You can say your answer aloud or write it on a separate piece of paper.

1. Where do you go to buy a new pair of shoes?
2. Where is the place to catch a train or subway?
3. Where can you find a menu and order food to eat?
4. Where do you keep your clothes when you're not wearing them?
5. Where can you see animals like lions, tigers, and bears?
6. Where do you usually wait for your luggage at the airport?
7. Where is a good spot to watch the stars at night?
8. Where do you find ingredients to make a sandwich?
9. Where can you find bicycles for rent?
10. Where do you often go to watch sporting events?
11. Where is a location to store your favorite books?
12. Where can you see aquatic animals like dolphins and sharks?
13. Where do you go when you need to withdraw cash?
14. Where can you find tools for fixing things around the house?
15. Where is a place to take a relaxing bath?
16. Where do you usually wait for your food at a restaurant?
17. Where can you find a wide range of electronics and gadgets?
18. Where is a common place to study or read quietly?
19. Where do you go when you need to renew your driver's license?
20. Where can you see art and artifacts from different cultures?
21. Where is a spot to enjoy a hot cup of coffee or tea?
22. Where do you often gather for family celebrations?
23. Where can you find toys and games for children?
24. Where is a location to admire historical buildings and sites?
25. Where do you usually wait for a friend before going out?

"Where" Questions

Answer each question with a single word or a brief phrase that best fits the question.
You can say your answer aloud or write it on a separate piece of paper.

1. Where do you go to see a doctor when you're not feeling well?
2. Where is the place to enjoy a sandy beach and ocean waves?
3. Where can you find fresh fruits and vegetables to buy?
4. Where do you often store your personal documents and files?
5. Where can you see exotic animals like giraffes and zebras?
6. Where do you usually board a plane for your vacation?
7. Where is a great place to have a picnic with family and friends?
8. Where do you find materials for DIY craft projects?
9. Where can you watch live performances and concerts?
10. Where do you typically put dirty laundry before washing it?
11. Where is a location to enjoy a scenic mountain view?
12. Where can you find a variety of delicious desserts?
13. Where do you go to deposit money into your bank account?
14. Where can you find stationery and office supplies?
15. Where is a spot to take a refreshing shower?
16. Where do you usually dine when celebrating a special occasion?
17. Where can you buy the latest fashion clothing and shoes?
18. Where is a common place to have quiet reflection and prayer?
19. Where do you go to get your car repaired or serviced?
20. Where can you see precious gems and jewelry on display?
21. Where is a place to savor gourmet cuisine and fine dining?
22. Where do you often gather with friends for social events?
23. Where can you find toys and games for all ages?
24. Where is a location to explore science and technology exhibits?
25. Where do you usually meet someone for a blind date?

"Who" Questions

Answer each question with a single word or a brief phrase that best fits the question. You can say your answer aloud or write it on a separate piece of paper.

1. Who starred as the boy who in the Harry Potter series?
2. Who formulated the theory of general relativity?
3. Who conducts experiments in a lab wearing a white coat?
4. Who serves and takes orders in a restaurant?
5. Who sang hits like "Thriller" and "Billie Jean"?
6. Who played Jack Dawson in the movie Titanic?
7. Who portrayed Batman in The Dark Knight trilogy?
8. Who cares for patients in a hospital wearing a white coat?
9. Who authored classics like Pride and Prejudice?
10. Who invented the telephone?
11. Who portrayed Jack Sparrow in Pirates of the Caribbean?
12. Who discovered the laws of motion?
13. Who hosts cooking shows wearing a chef's hat?
14. Who walked on the moon as an astronaut?
15. Who contributed to computer technology?
16. Who wrote The Cat in the Hat and Green Eggs and Ham?
17. Who painted the Mona Lisa and other masterpieces?
18. Who played James Bond in numerous films?
19. Who leads soccer teams and scores goals on the field?
20. Who delivered the "I Have a Dream" speech?
21. Who directed films like E.T. and Jurassic Park?
22. Who became Indiana Jones, the archaeologist?
23. Who played guitar and wrote "Purple Haze"?
24. Who performed daring escape acts and illusions?
25. Who presides over court proceedings in a judicial robe?

"Who" Questions

Answer each question with a single word or a brief phrase that best fits the question. You can say your answer aloud or write it on a separate piece of paper.

1. Who starred as the boy who in the "Harry Potter" series?
2. Who formulated the theory of general relativity?
3. Who conducts experiments in a lab wearing a white coat?
4. Who serves and takes orders in a restaurant?
5. Who sang hits like "Thriller" and "Billie Jean"?
6. Who played Jack Dawson in the movie "Titanic"?
7. Who portrayed Batman in "The Dark Knight" trilogy?
8. Who cares for patients in a hospital wearing a white coat?
9. Who authored classics like "Pride and Prejudice"?
10. Who invented the telephone?
11. Who portrayed Jack Sparrow in "Pirates of the Caribbean"?
12. Who discovered the laws of motion?
13. Who hosts cooking shows wearing a chef's hat?
14. Who walked on the moon as an astronaut?
15. Who contributed to computer technology?
16. Who wrote "The Cat in the Hat" and "Green Eggs and Ham"?
17. Who painted the "Mona Lisa" and other masterpieces?
18. Who played James Bond in numerous films?
19. Who leads soccer teams and scores goals on the field?
20. Who delivered the "I Have a Dream" speech?
21. Who directed films like "E.T." and "Jurassic Park"?
22. Who became Indiana Jones, the archaeologist?
23. Who played guitar and wrote "Purple Haze"?
24. Who performed daring escape acts and illusions?
25. Who presides over court proceedings in a judicial robe?

"Who" Questions

Answer each question with a single word or a brief phrase that best fits the question. You can say your answer aloud or write it on a separate piece of paper.

1. Who starred as the boy who in the Harry Potter series?
2. Who formulated the theory of general relativity?
3. Who conducts experiments in a lab wearing a white coat?
4. Who serves and takes orders in a restaurant?
5. Who sang hits like "Thriller" and "Billie Jean"?
6. Who played Jack Dawson in the movie Titanic?
7. Who portrayed Batman in The Dark Knight trilogy?
8. Who cares for patients in a hospital wearing a white coat?
9. Who authored classics like Pride and Prejudice?
10. Who invented the telephone?
11. Who portrayed Jack Sparrow in Pirates of the Caribbean?
12. Who discovered the laws of motion?
13. Who hosts cooking shows wearing a chef's hat?
14. Who walked on the moon as an astronaut?
15. Who contributed to computer technology?
16. Who wrote The Cat in the Hat and Green Eggs and Ham?
17. Who painted the Mona Lisa and other masterpieces?
18. Who played James Bond in numerous films?
19. Who leads soccer teams and scores goals on the field?
20. Who delivered the "I Have a Dream" speech?
21. Who directed films like E.T. and Jurassic Park?
22. Who became Indiana Jones, the archaeologist?
23. Who played guitar and wrote "Purple Haze"?
24. Who performed daring escape acts and illusions?
25. Who presides over court proceedings in a judicial robe?

"When" Questions

Answer each question with a single word or a brief phrase that best fits the question. You can say your answer aloud or write it on a separate piece of paper.

1. When do birds typically migrate for the winter?
2. When do you use an umbrella in the rain?
3. When is the best time to plant flowers in spring?
4. When do you celebrate your wedding anniversary?
5. When does the holiday season usually start?
6. When do you schedule a dentist appointment?
7. When is the ideal time for a beach vacation?
8. When do you light candles on a birthday cake?
9. When do you wear sunglasses on a sunny day?
10. When does daylight saving time begin in spring?
11. When do people usually exchange Christmas gifts?
12. When is the first day of the work week for most?
13. When do you take a break during the workday?
14. When does the school year typically end?
15. When is the best time for stargazing at night?
16. When do you put out cookies for Santa Claus?
17. When do you send holiday cards to loved ones?
18. When do you blow out candles on your cake?
19. When is the optimal time to plant vegetables?
20. When do you wear a costume for Halloween?
21. When do you watch fireworks on the Fourth of July?
22. When do you change your clocks in the fall?
23. When is a great time to enjoy ice cream?
24. When do you visit a pumpkin patch in autumn?
25. When do you schedule your annual checkup?

"When" Questions

Answer each question with a single word or a brief phrase that best fits the question.
You can say your answer aloud or write it on a separate piece of paper.

1. When do students typically have summer break?
2. When do you usually check your email during the day?
3. When is the best time for a picnic in the park?
4. When does the annual flower festival take place?
5. When do you turn on the heat in the winter?
6. When does the school day typically start?
7. When do you celebrate New Year's Eve?
8. When is the busiest shopping day of the year?
9. When do you start decorating for the holidays?
10. When do you schedule a meeting with colleagues?
11. When do you enjoy a cup of hot cocoa?
12. When is the ideal time for a family reunion?
13. When do you put up your Christmas tree?
14. When does the summer solstice occur?
15. When do you usually receive your paycheck?
16. When is the best time for a weekend getaway?
17. When do you send out party invitations?
18. When does the school year typically begin?
19. When do you enjoy a leisurely brunch?
20. When do you watch the sunrise in the morning?
21. When is the annual company picnic?
22. When do you start your spring cleaning?
23. When do you attend a wedding ceremony?
24. When is the perfect time for a road trip?
25. When do you plan your summer vacation?

"Why" Questions

Answer each question with a single word or a brief phrase that best fits the question.
You can say your answer aloud or write it on a separate piece of paper.

1. Why do birds sing in the morning?
2. Why is the sky blue during the day?
3. Why do leaves change color in the fall?
4. Why does water boil at a high temperature?
5. Why do people celebrate birthdays?
6. Why is the grass green in the spring?
7. Why do we have seasons on Earth?
8. Why do candles flicker in the wind?
9. Why is the ocean salty?
10. Why do we need to sleep at night?
11. Why are rainbows so colorful?
12. Why do people make wishes on stars?
13. Why does the moon change its shape?
14. Why are fireworks bright and colorful?
15. Why do we use umbrellas when it rains?
16. Why is the snow white in the winter?
17. Why do dogs wag their tails?
18. Why do people blow out birthday candles?
19. Why are some fruits sweet and others sour?
20. Why do birds migrate during the winter?
21. Why do we wear sunscreen at the beach?
22. Why does thunder follow lightning?
23. Why do flowers bloom in the spring?
24. Why are icicles long and pointy?
25. Why do clocks have hands that move?

"Why" Questions

Answer each question with a single word or a brief phrase that best fits the question. You can say your answer aloud or write it on a separate piece of paper.

1. Why do we need to eat?
2. Why is the sky blue during the day?
3. Why do birds sing in the morning?
4. Why do flowers bloom in spring?
5. Why do we wear sunscreen at the beach?
6. Why does ice float in water?
7. Why do dogs wag their tails?
8. Why do we brush our teeth?
9. Why do we use umbrellas when it rains?
10. Why do leaves fall off trees in autumn?
11. Why do we say "please" and "thank you"?
12. Why do we have seasons?
13. Why do we need to sleep?
14. Why do some animals hibernate?
15. Why do we celebrate birthdays?
16. Why do people smile when they're happy?
17. Why do we have different time zones?
18. Why do candles flicker?
19. Why do we use calendars?
20. Why do we laugh when something is funny?
21. Why do we have traffic lights?
22. Why do clouds form in the sky?
23. Why do we need to drink water?
24. Why do we see rainbows after rain?
25. Why do we have dreams when we sleep?

"Why" Questions

Answer each question with a single word or a brief phrase that best fits the question. You can say your answer aloud or write it on a separate piece of paper.

1. Why do we yawn?
2. Why are rainbows colorful?
3. Why do we have birthdays?
4. Why do we wear hats in the sun?
5. Why do fireflies glow at night?
6. Why do we say "goodbye"?
7. Why do we have dreams?
8. Why do ice cream cones melt?
9. Why do cats purr?
10. Why do we use cell phones?
11. Why do stars twinkle?
12. Why do we write with pens?
13. Why do we have holidays?
14. Why do birds migrate?
15. Why do we blow out candles?
16. Why do we need to exercise?
17. Why do dogs bark?
18. Why do we have traffic signs?
19. Why do we plant seeds?
20. Why do we use passwords?
21. Why do clocks have hands?
22. Why do we shake hands?
23. Why do we need oxygen?
24. Why do we have a moon?
25. Why do we learn new things?

"How" Questions

Answer each question with a single word or a brief phrase that best fits the question. You can say your answer aloud or write it on a separate piece of paper.

1. How does a bicycle move?
2. How do plants grow?
3. How do we hear sounds?
4. How do clouds form?
5. How does a rainbow appear?
6. How do we make ice?
7. How do bees make honey?
8. How does a clock work?
9. How do birds fly?
10. How does a computer work?
11. How do we breathe?
12. How does the sun rise?
13. How do we see colors?
14. How do magnets attract?
15. How does a camera take pictures?
16. How do trees get water?
17. How do we feel emotions?
18. How does a boat float?
19. How do birds build nests?
20. How do we taste food?
21. How does a flashlight shine?
22. How do we send emails?
23. How does electricity work?
24. How do we make paper?
25. How does a volcano erupt?

"How" Questions

Answer each question with a single word or a brief phrase that best fits the question. You can say your answer aloud or write it on a separate piece of paper.

1. How do we measure time?
2. How does a car move?
3. How do plants get energy?
4. How does water freeze?
5. How do we cook food?
6. How does a ball bounce?
7. How do stars twinkle?
8. How does a magnet work?
9. How do clouds float?
10. How do we write letters?
11. How does a phone ring?
12. How do we make music?
13. How does a kite fly?
14. How do leaves change colors?
15. How does a boat sail?
16. How do we count numbers?
17. How does a rainbow form?
18. How do animals hibernate?
19. How do we tie shoelaces?
20. How does a flower bloom?
21. How do we brush teeth?
22. How does a plane fly?
23. How do clocks tick?
24. How does fire burn?
25. How do we solve puzzles?

"How" Questions

Answer each question with a single word or a brief phrase that best fits the question. You can say your answer aloud or write it on a separate piece of paper.

1. How do you tie shoes?
2. How does a bird fly?
3. How do you make lemonade?
4. How does a clock tick?
5. How do you write your name?
6. How does a door open?
7. How do you set the table?
8. How does a boat float?
9. How do you brush teeth?
10. How does a car start?
11. How do you wash hands?
12. How does a ball bounce?
13. How do you cook eggs?
14. How does a light switch work?
15. How do you plant flowers?
16. How does a phone ring?
17. How do you bake bread?
18. How does a fan cool air?
19. How do you make a sandwich?
20. How does a kite fly?
21. How do you draw a smile?
22. How does a mirror reflect?
23. How do you ride a bike?
24. How does a faucet run water?
25. How do you read a book?

IDIOMATIC SENTENCES

Idiomatic Sentences Instructions

Objective:
To understand and interpret the figurative meaning of idiomatic expressions.

How This Exercise Helps:
This task helps in grasping non-literal language nuances, which is crucial for effective communication, especially in social contexts.

Instructions:
Review the Idiom: Read the idiomatic sentence provided. Example: "He has a heart of gold."

Interpret the Meaning: Say aloud or write a brief explanation of the idiom's figurative meaning. For the example, you could explain, "He is very kind and generous."

Assess Your Explanation: Ensure that your interpretation correctly conveys the idiom's essence.

Continue the Process: Move to the next sentence and repeat the steps to understand each idiom's figurative meaning.

Tips: Think about what the idiom might mean in everyday situations. Keep explanations simple and direct. If you're unfamiliar with the idiom, try to infer the meaning from context or familiar words within it.

Idiomatic Sentences

Explain the meaning of each idiomatic sentence in a few words or a short phrase.
You can say your answer aloud or write it on a separate piece of paper.

1. She does not have a green thumb.
2. I paid an arm and a leg for my new Tesla.
3. You're really in the hot seat over your mistake.
4. Butch's bark is worse than his bite.
5. Mr. Moody looks down on people who live in the city.
6. A stitch in time saves nine.
7. Don't spill the beans about Jennifer's engagement.
8. I'm shaking like a leaf about having to give a speech.
9. This steak dinner is on me.
10. I woke up on the wrong side of the bed today.
11. The grass is always greener on the other side of the fence.
12. Those kids are driving me up a tree.
13. Time flies when you're having fun.
14. George is a real wet blanket.
15. My boss really makes my blood boil.
16. All kinds of monkey business went on in the teacher's absence.
17. Don't count your chickens before they're hatched.
18. Alyssa is green with envy over my new car.
19. Don't let the cat out of the bag about the party.
20. She looks like a million bucks in that new dress.
21. His explanation was fishy.
22. The party was a piece of cake.
23. She's a tough cookie.
24. Bob is on cloud nine.
25. Mary's smile lights up the room.

Idiomatic Sentences

Explain the meaning of each idiomatic sentence in a few words or a short phrase.
You can say your answer aloud or write it on a separate piece of paper.

1. I'm feeling under the weather today.
2. They hit the nail on the head with that decision.
3. Don't cry over spilled milk.
4. Keep your chin up; things will get better.
5. Jeremy is a real couch potato.
6. They're just barking up the wrong tree.
7. She's a real bookworm.
8. We're all in the same boat.
9. Don't put all your eggs in one basket.
10. Bob is always a day late and a dollar short.
11. Her explanation was crystal clear.
12. We need to face the music about this problem.
13. The early bird catches the worm.
14. He's a snake in the grass.
15. You're walking on thin ice with that attitude.
16. We're in the same boat on this issue.
17. I'm just trying to break the ice.
18. It's a piece of cake to fix this.
19. They're a dime a dozen these days.
20. His plan is a double-edged sword.
21. She's a real night owl.
22. Don't put all your eggs in one basket.
23. He's a real jack of all trades.
24. You're skating on thin ice with that behavior.
25. She's a real firecracker in the office.

Idiomatic Sentences

Explain the meaning of each idiomatic sentence in a few words or a short phrase.
You can say your answer aloud or write it on a separate piece of paper.

1. His optimism is like a breath of fresh air.
2. He's trying to have his cake and eat it too.
3. We're all on the same page about the project.
4. She's really pulling your leg with that story.
5. It's time to face the music and admit the truth.
6. I can't wait to hit the hay after a long day.
7. He's a real pain in the neck at the meetings.
8. She's walking on air since she got the news.
9. He's barking up the wrong tree with that idea.
10. You're in hot water if you don't finish that report.
11. I'll cross that bridge when I come to it.
12. They're all ears about the surprise party.
13. He's just a small fish in a big pond.
14. We're all in the same boat regarding the deadline.
15. I'm over the moon about the promotion.
16. She's a real people person at the office.
17. You're opening a can of worms with that topic.
18. It's like finding a needle in a haystack.
19. He's a real whiz in the kitchen.
20. Don't let the cat out of the bag about the surprise.
21. We're all singing the same tune on this issue.
22. I can't believe he sold me down the river.
23. She's been riding his coattails for years.
24. It's like looking for a needle in a haystack.
25. I'm just trying to catch my breath after that run.

ANALOGIES

Analogy Exercise Instructions

Objective:
To develop reasoning skills by identifying relationships between pairs of words and completing analogies.

How This Exercise Helps:
Analogy exercises strengthen cognitive abilities by encouraging you to make connections between concepts and to understand word relationships, which is an important aspect of language and thought processing.

Instructions:
Understand the Relationship:

Complete the Analogy: Based on the first relationship, find the word that completes the second pair. Following the example above, since food satisfies hunger, water satisfies _______. The answer would be "thirst."

Reflect on Your Answer: Confirm that the completed analogy makes sense and that the relationships are parallel.

Progress to the Next Item: Continue with the subsequent analogies, applying the same process to deduce the relationships and complete them.

Tips:
Focus on the function or characteristic that links the first pair of words. Use that relationship as a guide for finding the correct word to complete the second pair. If you're uncertain, try forming a sentence with the words to see if it clarifies the relationship.

Analogies

Fill in the comparison with the correct word that completes each analogy.

1. FOOD is to HUNGRY as WATER is to _______________________
2. BABY is to YOUNG as GRANDPA is to _______________________
3. HAT is to HEAD as SHOES are to _______________________
4. A LOT is to A LITTLE as MORE is to _______________________
5. HARD is to SOFT as BUMPY is to _______________________
6. ELEPHANT is to BIG as MOUSE is to _______________________
7. BLUE is to SKY as GREEN is to _______________________
8. BED is to SLEEP as COUCH is to _______________________
9. POT is to PAN as BOWL is to _______________________
10. NICE is to MEAN as HAPPY is to _______________________
11. GENTLE is to KIND as GRUFF is to _______________________
12. WINTER is to COLD as SUMMER is to _______________________
13. BOOK is to READ as MOVIE is to _______________________
14. CAT is to MEOW as DOG is to _______________________
15. CLOCK is to TICK as CAR is to _______________________
16. SUN is to DAY as MOON is to _______________________
17. APPLE is to FRUIT as CARROT is to _______________________
18. FLOWER is to PETAL as TREE is to _______________________
19. PEN is to WRITE as PENCIL is to _______________________
20. OCEAN is to WATER as DESERT is to _______________________
21. DOCTOR is to MEDICINE as CHEF is to _______________________
22. FIRE is to HOT as ICE is to _______________________
23. DANCE is to MUSIC as BOOK is to _______________________
24. SOCCER is to SPORT as ART is to _______________________
25. RABBIT is to HOP as FISH is to _______________________

Analogies

Fill in the comparison with the correct word that completes each analogy.

1. SNAKE is to REPTILE as SPARROW is to _______________________

2. CAKE is to BAKE as SOUP is to _______________________

3. SWIM is to WATER as SKATE is to _______________________

4. GUITAR is to STRINGS as PIANO is to _______________________

5. SUNFLOWER is to YELLOW as APPLE is to _______________________

6. SAILBOAT is to OCEAN as KITE is to _______________________

7. LAUGHTER is to HAPPY as TEARS are to _______________________

8. TELEPHONE is to CALL as COMPUTER is to _______________________

9. SPRINT is to FAST as CRAWL is to _______________________

10. SCISSORS is to CUT as GLUE is to _______________________

11. ROSE is to FLOWER as CARROT is to _______________________

12. HORSE is to GALLOP as FISH is to _______________________

13. RAINBOW is to COLORS as GRAY is to _______________________

14. BALLOON is to FLOAT as ROCK is to _______________________

15. CANDLE is to FLAME as ELECTRICITY is to _______________________

16. DRUM is to BEAT as TRUMPET is to _______________________

17. MOON is to NIGHT as SUN is to _______________________

18. BIKE is to PEDAL as CAR is to _______________________

19. BUTTERFLY is to WINGS as SNAKE is to _______________________

20. LAUGHTER is to JOKE as APPLAUSE is to _______________________

21. RIVER is to FLOW as GLACIER is to _______________________

22. BARK is to DOG as MEOW is to _______________________

23. BEE is to BUZZ as LION is to _______________________

24. CAVE is to DARK as BEACH is to _______________________

25. AIRPLANE is to FLY as SUBMARINE is to _______________________

Analogies

Fill in the comparison with the correct word that completes each analogy.

1. PEN is to WRITE as KNIFE is to ______________________________

2. TEACHER is to SCHOOL as DOCTOR is to ______________________

3. SWEET is to SUGAR as SOUR is to ____________________________

4. FISH is to SWIM as BIRD is to ______________________________

5. SHOE is to FOOT as GLOVE is to _____________________________

6. WHEEL is to BICYCLE as TIRE is to __________________________

7. SEED is to PLANT as EGG is to ______________________________

8. SUN is to BRIGHT as NIGHT is to ____________________________

9. PAINTER is to BRUSH as WRITER is to ________________________

10. LEAF is to TREE as PETAL is to _____________________________

11. BREAD is to BAKE as SOUP is to _____________________________

12. SINGER is to MICROPHONE as PHOTOGRAPHER is to ____________

13. RAIN is to UMBRELLA as SUN is to ___________________________

14. MOUSE is to CAT as FISH is to ______________________________

15. HEART is to LOVE as BRAIN is to ____________________________

16. COFFEE is to CUP as SOUP is to _____________________________

17. SHADOW is to LIGHT as ECHO is to ___________________________

18. STARS are to NIGHT as CLOUDS are to ________________________

19. SALTY is to SEA as FRESH is to _____________________________

20. BOOK is to READ as SONG is to ______________________________

21. FIRE is to HOT as ICE is to ________________________________

22. NURSE is to PATIENT as TEACHER is to _______________________

23. LEAVES are to WIND as WAVES are to _________________________

24. KING is to THRONE as JUDGE is to ___________________________

25. MONEY is to BANK as BOOKS are to ___________________________

Analogies

Fill in the comparison with the correct word that completes each analogy.

1. DIAMOND is to JEWEL as PEARL is to ___________________________

2. BICYCLE is to WHEELS as CAR is to ___________________________

3. SWEATER is to WARM as ICE CREAM is to ___________________________

4. PENCIL is to WRITE as ERASER is to ___________________________

5. NIGHT is to DARKNESS as DAY is to ___________________________

6. SHARK is to OCEAN as LION is to ___________________________

7. POETRY is to WORDS as ART is to ___________________________

8. FRUIT is to ORCHARD as VEGETABLE is to ___________________________

9. WHISPER is to QUIET as SHOUT is to ___________________________

10. SUNRISE is to MORNING as SUNSET is to ___________________________

11. NOVEL is to BOOK as MOVIE is to ___________________________

12. BIRD is to NEST as SPIDER is to ___________________________

13. MAPLE is to LEAF as OAK is to ___________________________

14. THUNDER is to STORM as LIGHTNING is to ___________________________

15. LAUGHTER is to HAPPINESS as TEARS are to ___________________________

16. CHEF is to COOK as PILOT is to ___________________________

17. FLOWER is to PETALS as PINEAPPLE is to ___________________________

18. BEE is to HIVE as ANT is to ___________________________

19. FISH is to SWIM as BIRD is to ___________________________

20. CRAYON is to COLOR as CHARCOAL is to ___________________________

21. HOSPITAL is to HEALTH as LIBRARY is to ___________________________

22. WIND is to BREEZE as HURRICANE is to ___________________________

23. GUITAR is to STRINGS as PIANO is to ___________________________

24. CAMERA is to PICTURE as MICROSCOPE is to ___________________________

25. SAILBOAT is to WATER as BICYCLE is to ___________________________

Analogies

Fill in the comparison with the correct word that completes each analogy.

---

1. DAY is to SUNLIGHT as NIGHT is to _____________________
2. SHOES are to FEET as HAT is to _____________________
3. RAIN is to UMBRELLA as SUN is to _____________________
4. SALT is to SALTY as SUGAR is to _____________________
5. SNAKE is to REPTILE as SPARROW is to _____________________
6. HEART is to LOVE as BRAIN is to _____________________
7. FISH is to SWIM as BIRD is to _____________________
8. TREE is to FOREST as STAR is to _____________________
9. TEACHER is to SCHOOL as DOCTOR is to _____________________
10. PAINTBRUSH is to PAINTING as PEN is to _____________________
11. CLOCK is to TIME as THERMOMETER is to _____________________
12. LEAF is to TREE as PETAL is to _____________________
13. MOUSE is to CAT as FISH is to _____________________
14. COAL is to FIRE as SEED is to _____________________
15. KNIFE is to CUT as HAMMER is to _____________________
16. BOOK is to READ as SONG is to _____________________
17. BEE is to HONEY as COW is to _____________________
18. WHEEL is to BICYCLE as HEEL is to _____________________
19. WINTER is to COLD as SUMMER is to _____________________
20. SOUP is to SPOON as STEAK is to _____________________
21. OWL is to NIGHT as FALCON is to _____________________
22. WHISPER is to QUIET as SHOUT is to _____________________
23. NURSE is to HOSPITAL as TEACHER is to _____________________
24. BUTTERFLY is to CATERPILLAR as FROG is to _____________________
25. GLOVES are to HANDS as SOCKS are to _____________________

Yes / No Questions

Yes/No Questions Exercise Instructions

Objective:

To improve comprehension and response accuracy to questions that can be answered with a simple "Yes" or "No."

How This Exercise Helps:

This activity encourages decision-making based on understanding the content of questions. It also aids in processing speed as the answer requires only a one-word response, which is a common form of daily communication.

Instructions:

Review the Question: Read each question provided in your workbook carefully.

Determine Your Response: Decide if the answer to the question is "Yes" or "No" based on the information given or common knowledge.

Indicate Your Answer: Write down or say "Yes" or "No" as your answer to each question.

Reflect on Your Decision: After answering, take a moment to consider why you chose "Yes" or "No" and whether the question could be ambiguous.

Tip: Think about the question context; sometimes the answer may not be immediately obvious. Remember that some questions may be tricky or have a less clear-cut answer; use your best judgment. Practice saying your answers aloud if possible, to aid in speech fluency.

Yes / No Questions

Answer each question with either "Yes" or "No."

1. Is the sun bigger than the moon?
2. Can fish fly in the air?
3. Do birds have feathers?
4. Is the ocean made of chocolate?
5. Can you swim in a pool?
6. Are bicycles used for underwater travel?
7. Can you eat a shoe?
8. Is a car faster than a snail?
9. Do cats bark like dogs?
10. Are elephants smaller than ants?
11. Can you hear sound in space?
12. Is the sky usually green?
13. Can you breathe underwater without equipment?
14. Are apples a type of fruit?
15. Can you taste with your eyes?
16. Do dogs have tails?
17. Is the Earth flat?
18. Can you see in the dark?
19. Are books made from trees?
20. Is ice cream hot?
21. Do people have ten fingers?
22. Can you see the stars during the day?
23. Is sand typically found at the beach?
24. Can you hear music on the radio?
25. Is the moon made of cheese?

Yes / No Questions

Answer each question with either "Yes" or "No."

1. Can a fish live out of water?
2. Is the color orange named after the fruit?
3. Do penguins fly?
4. Is a tomato a fruit?
5. Can some birds talk?
6. Is basketball played with a bat?
7. Do all snakes have venom?
8. Can humans breathe underwater without equipment?
9. Is a dolphin a type of fish?
10. Do cacti grow in the desert?
11. Is the moon a planet?
12. Can cars run without fuel?
13. Do elephants have wings?
14. Is it possible for humans to hear ultrasonic sounds?
15. Can kangaroos walk backwards?
16. Is ice cream warm?
17. Does the sun rise in the west?
18. Can cheetahs climb trees?
19. Is snow black?
20. Do ostriches bury their heads in the sand when scared?
21. Can a person sneeze with their eyes open?
22. Is Mount Everest the tallest mountain in the world?
23. Can all birds swim?
24. Is it safe to look directly at the sun?
25. Do bees produce honey?

Yes / No Questions

Answer each question with either "Yes" or "No."

1. Can you ride a bicycle underwater?
2. Is the sky green at night?
3. Do giraffes have short necks?
4. Can you breathe in outer space?
5. Are bananas a type of vegetable?
6. Do frogs say "meow"?
7. Is a car slower than a snail?
8. Can you eat a table?
9. Does snow fall in summer?
10. Are elephants smaller than mice?
11. Can you hear silence?
12. Are mountains flat?
13. Can you swim in a desert?
14. Is the sun made of cheese?
15. Do fish fly like birds?
16. Can you touch a rainbow?
17. Are clouds made of cotton candy?
18. Can you live without water?
19. Do kangaroos hop on their heads?
20. Is the North Pole in Antarctica?
21. Can you see through walls?
22. Are whales smaller than goldfish?
23. Is a computer faster than a cheetah?
24. Can you eat the moon?
25. Does water flow uphill?

Yes / No Questions

Answer each question with either "Yes" or "No."

1. Is the Earth flat?

2. Can you hear colors?

3. Does chocolate taste better than ice cream?

4. Are cows purple?

5. Can you touch a rainbow?

6. Is the moon made of cheese?

7. Can you swim in the desert?

8. Do fish fly like birds?

9. Is water transparent?

10. Can you travel back in time?

11. Does sugar taste salty?

12. Are polar bears found in the desert?

13. Can you see through walls?

14. Are clouds made of candy?

15. Is sandpaper smooth?

16. Can you eat the sun?

17. Do cats bark like dogs?

18. Is the sky green?

19. Can you jump to the moon?

20. Does fire freeze?

21. Are mountains made of chocolate?

22. Can you breathe underwater?

23. Is the ocean made of lemonade?

24. Do rocks float in the air?

25. Can you taste sound?

Yes / No Questions

Answer each question with either "Yes" or "No."

1. Is chocolate made from cocoa beans?
2. Can a vegetarian eat chicken?
3. Does the human body have more than one brain?
4. Are there rings around Saturn?
5. Can a square have rounded corners?
6. Is a jellyfish considered a type of fish?
7. Do all mammals lay eggs?
8. Can ostriches fly?
9. Is bamboo a type of wood?
10. Do all flowers bloom during the day?
11. Is a koala a bear species?
12. Can a human outrun a horse in a marathon?
13. Does the heart stop when you sneeze?
14. Is it possible to see air?
15. Can a frog live both in water and on land?
16. Are spiders insects?
17. Do bats have good eyesight?
18. Is it possible for a cat to bark?
19. Can turtles come out of their shells?
20. Is Spanish spoken in Brazil as the official language?
21. Can lightning strike the same place twice?
22. Is the Great Wall of China visible from space?
23. Do all dogs have tails?
24. Is the Sahara Desert the largest desert in the world?
25. Can humans drink seawater to stay hydrated?

Location Questions

Locations Questions Exercise Instructions

Objective:
To enhance geographical knowledge and recall by identifying and articulating answers to location-based questions.

How This Exercise Helps:
This exercise strengthens cognitive mapping and memory recall related to geography, which are useful for daily navigation and learning about different regions.

Instructions:
Read the Question Carefully: Focus on the location-related question provided in your workbook.

Determine the Correct Location: Use your knowledge to find the appropriate answer or feel free to research if necessary.

Respond with Your Answer: Say your answer aloud to practice verbal skills or write it down on a separate piece of paper to reinforce memory retention.

Review Your Answers: Go back over your responses to make sure they are accurate and correct any that aren't.

Tips:
Consider the type of place in the question (Is it a city, country, continent, or landmark?). If the answer doesn't come to you immediately, use association techniques with related places or landmarks.   Practicing out loud can help with speech fluency, while writing responses can aid in written language recall.

Location Questions

Answer these general knowledge questions about locations.

1. What country is to the north of the United States?
2. Where is Mexico located?
3. Is Scotland part of the United Kingdom?
4. Name one southern state in the United States.
5. Name a city on the West Coast of the United States.
6. Where is the Great Salt Lake located?
7. In which U.S. state will you find The Grand Canyon?
8. Name a city situated on one of the Great Lakes.
9. What is the largest state in the U.S.?
10. What is the smallest state in the U.S.?
11. Name a major Canadian city.
12. Is Egypt in Africa?
13. Are the Philippines located off the coast of South America?
14. Name a country that consists entirely of islands.
15. Where is the city of Sydney located?
16. In which country can you find Tokyo?
17. Rome is the capital of which country?
18. St. Petersburg and Kiev are major cities in what country?
19. In which mountain range can you find Mount Everest?
20. Ethiopia is located on which continent?
21. What country is south of Canada?
22. Where is the Sahara Desert?
23. Name a city in South America.
24. What country is known as the Land of the Rising Sun?
25. Where is the Eiffel Tower located?

Location Questions

Answer these general knowledge questions about locations.

1. What is the capital of California?
2. Name a state that borders Texas.
3. In which state is Yellowstone National Park located?
4. Which river forms the border between Texas and Mexico?
5. What is the tallest mountain in the contiguous United States?
6. Where is the Statue of Liberty located?
7. What is the largest city in Illinois?
8. Name a state that has a coastline on the Pacific Ocean.
9. Which state is known as the "Sunshine State"?
10. In which state can you find the Grand Canyon?
11. What is the largest city in Texas?
12. Which state is famous for its potatoes?
13. Name a state that is part of New England.
14. In which state can you visit Mount Rushmore?
15. What is the capital of New York?
16. Where is the Kennedy Space Center located?
17. Which state is often called the "Last Frontier"?
18. Name a state that is known for its maple syrup production.
19. In which state is the Alamo located?
20. What is the highest peak in the Rocky Mountains?
21. Where is the Hollywood Walk of Fame?
22. Which state is famous for its lobster?
23. In which state is the Hoover Dam located?
24. What is the largest city in Florida?
25. Name the state known as the "Land of Enchantment."

Location Questions

Answer these general knowledge questions about locations.

1. What is the capital of Nevada?
2. Name a state that is part of the Pacific Northwest.
3. In which state can you visit the Everglades National Park?
4. Which river flows through the Grand Canyon?
5. What is the largest lake in the United States by surface area?
6. Where is the Gateway Arch located?
7. What is the capital of Ohio?
8. Name a state that borders Missouri.
9. Which state is known as the "Land of 10,000 Lakes"?
10. In which state is Yosemite National Park situated?
11. What is the capital of New Jersey?
12. Which state is famous for its potatoes?
13. Name a state that is part of the Four Corners region.
14. In which state can you find the Great Smoky Mountains?
15. What is the largest city in Pennsylvania?
16. Where is the United States Naval Academy located?
17. Which state is often referred to as "The Volunteer State"?
18. Name a state that is part of the Appalachian Mountains.
19. In which state can you explore Bryce Canyon National Park?
20. What is the capital of Indiana?
21. Where is the Rock and Roll Hall of Fame situated?
22. Which state is famous for its blueberries?
23. In which state is the Space Needle located?
24. What is the largest city in Michigan?
25. Name the state known as the "Sunflower State."

Location Questions

Answer these general knowledge questions about locations.

1. What is the capital of France?
2. Where is the Great Barrier Reef located?
3. In which country would you find Mount Fuji?
4. What is the largest continent?
5. Which river runs through Egypt?
6. What city is known as the Big Apple?
7. Where is the Taj Mahal?
8. In which country is the city of Barcelona?
9. What is the smallest country in the world?
10. Where would you find the Amazon Rainforest?
11. Which U.S. state is known as the "Sunshine State"?
12. What is the capital city of Australia?
13. Where are the Pyramids of Giza?
14. In which country is the city of Istanbul located?
15. What is the longest river in the world?
16. Which desert covers most of northern Africa?
17. Where is the Colosseum?
18. What is the capital of Canada?
19. Where is the highest mountain in North America located?
20. What ocean lies to the east of the United States?
21. Which U.S. state is known for Hollywood?
22. What is the name of the west of California?
23. Where is the ancient city of Petra located?
24. What is the capital of Japan?
25. In which city would you find the Acropolis?

Location Questions

Answer these general knowledge questions about locations.

1. What city is the Statue of Liberty in?
2. What country is the Eiffel Tower located in?
3. Where would you find kangaroos in the wild?
4. Which continent is Egypt part of?
5. What is the capital of the United Kingdom?
6. Where is the Golden Gate Bridge?
7. Which country is known for maple syrup?
8. Where are the Great Pyramids?
9. What river is in New York City?
10. What state is the Grand Canyon in?
11. Which ocean is off the California coast?
12. Where is the capital city, Ottawa?
13. What country is the Colosseum in?
14. What city is known as the City of Love?
15. Where is Mount Everest?
16. What is the largest state in the USA?
17. Where is the Amazon rainforest?
18. What country is the Taj Mahal in?
19. Where is the Great Barrier Reef?
20. Which sea is next to Italy?
21. What state is famous for Hollywood?
22. Where is the capital city, Tokyo?
23. Which country has a city named Vancouver?
24. What country is the largest in size?
25. Where is the city of Berlin?

History Questions

History Questions Exercise Instructions

Objective:
Recall significant historical figures, events, and facts through simple questions.

How This Exercise Helps:
Helps with memory recall and connecting to well-known historical information.

Instructions:
Read the Question: Look at the question and think about the answer.
Respond: Answer aloud or write your answer on a separate paper.
Check Answers: Review your answers to ensure they are accurate.

History Questions

Answer these general knowledge questions about history.
Say the answer aloud or write on a separate piece of paper.

Who was the first President of the United States?

In what year did World War II end?

Who was the first woman to fly solo across the Atlantic Ocean?

Which civilization built the pyramids in Egypt?

Who is credited with inventing the lightbulb?

What was the name of the wall that divided Berlin during the Cold War?

In what year did the Titanic sink?

Who discovered the antibiotic penicillin?

What was the name of the first powered airplane?

Who was the British monarch during the American Revolution?

What was the first capital of the United States?

Which ancient city was buried by the eruption of Mount Vesuvius in 79 AD?

Who painted the Mona Lisa?

Which country gifted the Statue of Liberty to the USA?

Who was the first person to walk on the moon?

What empire was ruled by Julius Caesar?

In what year was the United States Constitution signed?

What was the main trigger for World War I?

Who was known as the 'Mad Monk' in Russian history?

Which ancient civilization is credited with inventing the wheel?

Who was the longest-reigning British monarch before Queen Elizabeth II?

Which U.S. President abolished slavery?

What war was fought between the North and South in the USA?

Who was the first female Prime Minister of the United Kingdom?

What large stone structure did the Romans build across Great Britain?

History Questions

Answer these general knowledge questions about history.
Say the answer aloud or write on a separate piece of paper.

What city was the center of the Roman Empire?

Who was the main author of the U.S. Declaration of Independence?

What ancient structure is known for its hanging gardens?

Who was the Egyptian queen famous for her relationship with Mark Antony?

Where did the Renaissance begin?

Who was the Russian leader during World War II?

What year did the Berlin Wall fall?

What was the major conflict in the 1950s between North and South Korea called?

Who was the first female ruler of England?

What was the first permanent English settlement in America?

Who discovered the Americas in 1492?

What empire was Napoleon Bonaparte the emperor of?

What historical event is Guy Fawkes Night associated with?

Who was the inventor of the printing press?

What catastrophic event struck Europe in the mid-14th century?

Who was the leader of the Indian independence movement?

What was the main religion of the Aztec Empire?

Who was the first Roman Emperor?

In which war did the Battle of Gettysburg occur?

What ancient city-state was ruled by Pericles?

What famous document did Abraham Lincoln sign in 1863?

Who was the British Prime Minister during most of World War II?

Where was the ancient city of Carthage located?

Who was the famous female pharaoh of ancient Egypt?

What was the name of the ship on which the Pilgrims traveled to America?

History Questions

Answer these general knowledge questions about history.
Say the answer aloud or write on a separate piece of paper.

Who wrote the Declaration of Independence?

What year did World War II end?

Who was the first woman to fly solo across the Atlantic?

What ancient civilization built the pyramids?

Who invented the lightbulb?

What wall divided Berlin during the Cold War?

Which ship sank after hitting an iceberg in 1912?

Who discovered penicillin?

What was the name of the first successful airplane?

Who was the British monarch during the American Revolution?

What was the first capital of the United States?

What ancient city was buried by a volcanic eruption in 79 AD?

Who painted the Mona Lisa?

Which country gifted the Statue of Liberty to the USA?

Who was the first person to step on the moon?

What empire did Julius Caesar rule?

In which year was the United States Constitution signed?

What was the main cause of World War I?

Who was known as the 'Mad Monk' in Russian history?

What ancient civilization invented the wheel?

Who was the longest-reigning British monarch before Queen Elizabeth II?

Which president abolished slavery in the United States?

What war was fought between the North and South regions in the USA?

Who was the first female Prime Minister of the United Kingdom?

What famous structure did the Romans build across the UK?

History Questions

Answer these general knowledge questions about history.
Say the answer aloud or write on a separate piece of paper.

What ancient structure was built in China for protection?

Who led the Soviet Union during the Cuban Missile Crisis?

In which city was John F. Kennedy assassinated?

What was the main fighting style in the Trojan War?

Who was the first woman to rule China as emperor?

What country did Christopher Columbus sail for?

What ancient empire was centered in modern-day Peru?

Who was the second President of the United States?

Which war was fought between the British and Chinese over opium?

What was the primary language of the Roman Empire?

Who was the King of England during the American War of Independence?

What is the name of the battle where Napoleon was finally defeated?

Who was the famous nurse during the Crimean War?

What was the largest empire in history by land area?

Who was the famous scientist who developed the theory of relativity?

What is the name of the first known democracy in the world?

Who was the famous civil rights leader assassinated in 1968?

What famous structure did the Romans build to entertain citizens?

Who was the Greek god of war?

What empire did Alexander the Great inherit?

Which country was divided into East and West after World War II?

Who was the longest reigning monarch of the British Empire?

What is the oldest university in the United States?

Who discovered the polio vaccine?

What major world event took place from 1914 to 1918?

History Questions

Answer these general knowledge questions about history.
Say the answer aloud or write on a separate piece of paper.

In which city is the Louvre Museum located?

Who was the leader of Germany during World War I?

What ancient civilization is known for the Colosseum?

Who was the wife of President Franklin D. Roosevelt?

Which country gifted the Statue of Liberty to the USA?

Who discovered the laws of motion and gravity?

What was the main religion of the Roman Empire?

Who was the first emperor of Rome?

What country was Cleopatra queen of?

What historical period is known for the Black Plague?

Who was the first woman to fly across the English Channel?

What was the dominant empire in South America in the 15th century?

Who was the main leader of the Soviet Union during World War II?

What famous battle did William the Conqueror win in 1066?

Who was the Roman god of the sea?

What is the name of the first permanent English colony in America?

What war was Joan of Arc involved in?

Who was the first African American to play Major League Baseball?

What ancient civilization built Machu Picchu?

Who was the first human to travel into space?

What war did the United States fight in the 1960s and 1970s?

What ancient civilization is known for inventing the alphabet?

What large empire did Genghis Khan found?

Who was the queen of England during World War II?

What was the ancient Egyptian writing system called?

Popular Media Questions

Popular Media Questions Exercise Instructions

Objective:
To enhance knowledge and recall of popular media, including movies, music, TV shows, books, and games.

How This Exercise Helps:
This activity stimulates memory recall and encourages engagement with various aspects of popular culture, enhancing cognitive connections.

Instructions:
Read the Question: Focus on each media-related question provided.

Think About the Answer: Reflect on your knowledge of movies, music, TV shows, books, and games to find the answer.

Respond: Answer the question aloud or write your answer on a separate piece of paper.

Review: After answering, check your response for accuracy.

Tip: Relate the question to your personal experiences with media.
Don't rush; take your time to recall the information.
Discuss your answers with others to enhance engagement and enjoyment.

Popular Media Questions

Answer these general knowledge questions about history.
Say the answer aloud or write on a separate piece of paper.

1. What animated film features a young lion named Simba?
2. Who played James Bond in multiple movies?
3. Dorothy's famous shoe color in "The Wizard of Oz"?
4. Long-running TV series following the Simpson family?
5. Title of the first Harry Potter book?
6. Highest-grossing film of all time?
7. Author of "To Kill a Mockingbird"?
8. Name of Harry Potter's wizarding school?
9. Who is known as the "King of Pop" in the music industry?
10. Superhero with red cape and lasso of truth?
11. Famous phrase associated with "The Matrix" pills?
12. Magical land where toys come to life?
13. Director of "Lord of the Rings" trilogy?
14. Film about a young mermaid dreaming of life on land?
15. TV series about characters in a fictional hospital?
16. Name of Wookiee co-pilot in "Star Wars"?
17. Name of the magical school bus in an educational series?
18. Iconic detective with a pipe and deerstalker hat?
19. Classic novel with Elizabeth Bennet and Mr. Darcy?
20. Name of the magical school in J.K. Rowling's books?
21. Actor playing Hannibal Lecter in "The Silence of the Lambs"?
22. Title of the first book in Stephenie Meyer's "Twilight" series?
23. Disney film with a glass slipper and a pumpkin carriage?
24. Name of J.R.R. Tolkien's fictional wizard?
25. Phrase used for exploring new worlds in "Star Trek" series?

Popular Media Questions

Answer these general knowledge questions about history.
Say the answer aloud or write on a separate piece of paper.

1. Iconic actor known for "Dirty Harry" and "Million Dollar Baby"?
2. Name of Disney's animated movie featuring Elsa and Anna?
3. What TV show follows doctors at Grey Sloan Memorial Hospital?
4. Beloved wizard in a popular book series by J.K. Rowling?
5. Catchphrase used by Arnold Schwarzenegger in "The Terminator"?
6. Film series featuring young wizards battling the dark lord Voldemort?
7. Classic Disney film with a pumpkin carriage and glass slipper?
8. Actor who portrayed Jack Dawson in "Titanic"?
9. Main character who lives in a pineapple under the sea?
10. Author of the "A Song of Ice and Fire" book series?
11. Superhero known for his web-slinging abilities?
12. Renowned fantasy series adapted into a successful HBO show?
13. Acclaimed director behind "Pulp Fiction" and "Kill Bill"?
14. Disney character who loses her voice but gains legs?
15. Iconic detective created by Arthur Conan Doyle?
16. Famous director of the "Jurassic Park" and "E.T." films?
17. Alien film series with the tagline "In space, no one can hear you scream"?
18. Author of the "Hunger Games" trilogy?
19. Film series centered around a young wizard with a lightning bolt scar?
20. Actor known for roles in "Forrest Gump" and "Cast Away"?
21. Superhero with a red and gold suit built by Tony Stark?
22. TV series with a group of friends living in New York City?
23. Main character in a galaxy far, far away known for his Jedi abilities?
24. Award-winning fantasy series by George R.R. Martin?
25. Actress who portrayed Katniss Everdeen in "The Hunger Games" films?

History Questions

Answer these general knowledge questions about history.
Say the answer aloud or write on a separate piece of paper.

Who wrote the Declaration of Independence?

What year did World War II end?

Who was the first woman to fly solo across the Atlantic?

What ancient civilization built the pyramids?

Who invented the lightbulb?

What wall divided Berlin during the Cold War?

Which ship sank after hitting an iceberg in 1912?

Who discovered penicillin?

What was the name of the first successful airplane?

Who was the British monarch during the American Revolution?

What was the first capital of the United States?

What ancient city was buried by a volcanic eruption in 79 AD?

Who painted the Mona Lisa?

Which country gifted the Statue of Liberty to the USA?

Who was the first person to step on the moon?

What empire did Julius Caesar rule?

In which year was the United States Constitution signed?

What was the main cause of World War I?

Who was known as the 'Mad Monk' in Russian history?

What ancient civilization invented the wheel?

Who was the longest-reigning British monarch before Queen Elizabeth II?

Which president abolished slavery in the United States?

What war was fought between the North and South regions in the USA?

Who was the first female Prime Minister of the United Kingdom?

What famous structure did the Romans build across the UK?

Popular Media Questions

Answer these general knowledge questions about history.
Say the answer aloud or write on a separate piece of paper.

1. Who is the famous detective created by Sir Arthur Conan Doyle?
2. What is the highest-grossing movie of all time?
3. Who sang "Like a Virgin" and "Material Girl"?
4. What TV show features families named the Starks and Lannisters?
5. Who wrote the "Lord of the Rings" series?
6. Which movie features a character named Dorothy and a dog named Toto?
7. Who is the famous talk show host known for giving away cars?
8. What is the name of the animated movie with a lion named Simba?
9. Who played the lead role in the movie "Forrest Gump"?
10. In which movie do toys come to life when humans aren't around?
11. Name of the Disney movie about a puppet whose nose grows when he lies?
12. Who is the author of the "Harry Potter" book series?
13. What movie features a large ship that hits an iceberg?
14. Who is the famous cartoon sponge who lives in a pineapple under the sea?
15. What TV series is about four scientists in Pasadena?
16. Who is the superhero with a shield as his main weapon?
17. Which TV show features six friends living in New York City?
18. Who is the artist known for the album "Thriller"?
19. What movie features a love story on a ship called Titanic?
20. What TV show is known for the phrase "Winter is Coming"?
21. What popular video game series features a plumber trying to save a princess?
22. Who sang "Born This Way" and is known for her unique fashion?
23. Who is the famous singer behind the hit "Hello"?
24. Who wrote "Romeo and Juliet" and "Macbeth"?
25. Who wrote the detective novel "Murder on the Orient Express"?

Popular Media Questions

Answer these general knowledge questions about history.
Say the answer aloud or write on a separate piece of paper.

1. Who created "Star Wars"?
2. What movie features a shark named Bruce?
3. Who sang "Purple Rain"?
4. What's the TV series about a chemistry teacher turned criminal?
5. Who wrote "Charlie and the Chocolate Factory"?
6. What is the name of the green muscular superhero?
7. Who hosts "The Daily Show"?
8. What TV series is set in Westeros?
9. Who is the lead singer of U2?
10. What movie features dinosaurs on an island?
11. Who designed the first flag of the USA?
12. What's the TV show about plane crash survivors on an island?
13. Who directed "Jurassic Park"?
14. What movie is about boxing, starring Sylvester Stallone?
15. Who wrote "Pride and Prejudice"?
16. What band performed "Bohemian Rhapsody"?
17. What's the TV show featuring a high-functioning sociopath detective?
18. Who wrote "The Hobbit"?
19. What movie features a blue alien world called Pandora?
20. Who sang "La Bamba"?
21. What's the film where a ship hits an iceberg and sinks?
22. What TV show features the phrase "Bazinga"?
23. Who wrote "1984"?
24. What's the TV show about a group of friends in Manhattan?
25. What movie franchise features an archaeologist named Indiana Jones?

Memory

Answer the following questions about your own experiences. If you have a partner, recall and share your memories to stimulate conversation and connection.

1. What is your favorite childhood memory?
2. Can you recall the first book you ever read?
3. Do you remember your first day of school?
4. What's the most recent movie you watched, can you recall its plot?
5. What did you have for breakfast this morning?
6. Can you name the last three books you read?
7. Recall a memorable vacation destination you visited.
8. What's the name of your best childhood friend?
9. Do you remember your high school prom or other school dance?
10. Name three hobbies or activities you enjoyed in your younger years.
11. Think of a special family tradition you cherish.
12. Can you remember the lyrics to your favorite song?
13. What's the most recent gift you received, and from whom?
14. Recall the names of your closest neighbors or childhood neighbors.
15. What was the most recent restaurant you dined at, and what did you order?
16. Who was your favorite teacher in school, and why?
17. Can you recall your first pet's name and its species?
18. Name three memorable places you've lived throughout your life.
19. Think of a significant milestone or achievement you accomplished.
20. Do you remember your first job, and what was it?
21. Recall the title and author of a book that deeply impacted you.
22. Can you describe a particularly funny or embarrassing moment from your past?
23. What's the most recent book you recommended to someone, and why?
24. Think of a childhood game or activity you used to enjoy with friends.
25. Can you remember your earliest childhood dream or aspiration?

Memory

Answer the following questions about your own experiences. If you have a partner, recall and share your memories to stimulate conversation and connection.

1. What was the first concert you ever attended?
2. Which childhood toy do you have the fondest memories of?
3. What's the name of the first pet you ever had?
4. Can you recall the first book you read as a child?
5. What was the most memorable family vacation you've been on?
6. Do you remember the name of your favorite childhood teacher?
7. What was the first movie you watched in a theater?
8. What's the earliest childhood memory you can recall?
9. Can you describe the house you grew up in?
10. What's your favorite childhood game to play with friends?
11. What's the most memorable gift you've ever received?
12. Do you remember your first best friend's name?
13. Can you recall the first car you ever owned?
14. What's a significant achievement you accomplished in school?
15. What was the first job you had as a teenager?
16. Can you remember your first cell phone or smartphone?
17. What was your favorite subject in school and why?
18. Do you have a cherished family recipe from your childhood?
19. Can you recall a funny or embarrassing childhood moment?
20. What's a valuable lesson you learned from your parents or guardians?
21. What was your favorite childhood TV show or cartoon?
22. Can you remember the first time you rode a bicycle without training wheels?
23. What's a memorable holiday tradition from your family?
24. Do you recall a special childhood nickname you had?
25. What's a vivid memory from your high school graduation day?

Memory

Answer the following questions about your own experiences. If you have a partner, recall and share your memories to stimulate conversation and connection.

1. What was your first job ever, and what did you do?
2. Can you remember your favorite childhood bedtime story?
3. What's a memorable achievement or award you received in school?
4. Do you recall your first bicycle, and what color was it?
5. What's a place you visited during your childhood that left a lasting impression?
6. What was your favorite childhood board game to play with friends?
7. Can you describe the first home you lived in on your own?
8. What's a unique talent or hobby you had as a child?
9. Do you remember the first computer or video game you played?
10. What's a song that instantly transports you back to your teenage years?
11. Can you share a humorous or interesting story from your school days?
12. What was your dream career when you were a child?
13. Do you recall a special family tradition during holidays?
14. What's a memorable summer vacation from your youth?
15. Can you remember the name of your favorite childhood teacher?
16. What's a significant historical event that occurred during your childhood?
17. Share a vivid memory from your first day of school.
18. What's a memorable adventure you had with your siblings?
19. Can you describe your favorite childhood park or playground?
20. Share a valuable lesson you learned from a family member.
21. What's the first movie you ever watched in a movie theater?
22. Can you recall your first experience with snow or the beach?
23. What's a unique dish or food item you enjoyed as a child?
24. Share a story about a cherished family heirloom.
25. Can you remember your earliest childhood friend and their name?

Memory

Answer the following questions about your own experiences. If you have a partner, recall and share your memories to stimulate conversation and connection.

1. What's a significant event or achievement from your teenage years?
2. Can you recall your favorite childhood toy or stuffed animal?
3. Share a memorable story from a family gathering or reunion.
4. What's a life lesson you've learned from a challenging experience?
5. Do you remember your first pet's name and type of pet?
6. What's the earliest book you can remember reading as a child?
7. Share a humorous memory from your school days.
8. Can you describe the house you grew up in, including its color?
9. What's a fun childhood game you enjoyed playing with friends?
10. Do you recall a special meal or dish your parents used to make?
11. Share a story about a remarkable teacher or mentor you had.
12. What's the first concert or live performance you attended?
13. Can you remember your favorite childhood holiday tradition?
14. Share a memorable experience from a school field trip.
15. What's a hobby or interest you pursued in your early adult life?
16. Do you remember the first car you ever owned or drove?
17. Share a unique adventure or trip from your college years.
18. What's a favorite memory from your first job or workplace?
19. Can you recall a significant historical event during your youth?
20. Share a heartwarming story about your best childhood friend.
21. What's a piece of advice you received from a family member?
22. Do you remember your high school prom or a significant dance?
23. Share a memory related to learning a musical instrument.
24. What's a meaningful experience from your first apartment or home?
25. Can you describe your first experience flying in an airplane?

Safety Questions

Answer each safety-related question based on your knowledge and understanding of safety protocols. How would you respond or what actions would you take in each scenario?

1. How can you safely store household cleaning chemicals?

2. What steps can you take to prevent a kitchen grease fire?

3. How should you secure sliding glass doors against break-ins?

4. What's the safest way to use space heaters at home?

5. How can you childproof electrical outlets effectively?

6. What measures should be taken to secure heavy furniture?

7. How can you prevent slips and falls on staircases?

8. What's the proper maintenance for smoke detectors?

9. How should you prepare for a potential power outage?

10. What's the best way to protect your home against flooding?

11. What are the key aspects of home fire escape planning?

12. How can you secure your garage against theft?

13. What's the right approach to prevent carbon monoxide exposure?

14. How should you safely handle and store firearms?

15. What steps can you take to protect your home when traveling?

16. How to ensure your mail and packages are secure from theft?

17. What's the proper way to store firewood near your home?

18. How can you safeguard your home against extreme weather?

19. What's the safest way to use a generator during power outages?

20. How should you secure ladders to prevent accidents?

21. What measures can you take to protect your online privacy?

22. How can you secure your Wi-Fi network from hackers?

23. What's the safest approach to handle home renovation projects?

24. How to recognize and avoid common home repair scams?

25. What's the best way to dispose of hazardous household waste?

Safety Questions

Answer each safety-related question based on your knowledge and understanding of safety protocols. How would you respond or what actions would you take in each scenario?

1. What should you do if you smell gas in your home?
2. How often should you test your smoke alarms?
3. What is the safest way to extinguish a grease fire?
4. What should you do if there's an earthquake?
5. How should you behave when approaching a traffic light that's yellow?
6. What's the safest way to lift a heavy object?
7. How often should you replace your fire extinguisher?
8. What should you do if you encounter a bear in the wild?
9. What should you do if you break a glass?
10. What should you do if you get lost hiking?
11. How should you handle raw meat to avoid food poisoning?
12. What is the rule about swimming after eating?
13. How should you protect yourself during a thunderstorm?
14. What's the safest way to drive in foggy conditions?
15. How can you childproof electrical outlets?
16. What's the best way to stay safe in extreme heat?
17. How do you safely dispose of expired or unused medications?
18. How can you avoid frostbite in extremely cold weather?
19. What steps can you take to prevent mold growth in your home?
20. What's the first thing to do if someone is unresponsive?
21. How should you treat a minor burn?
22. What's the most important safety gear for a cyclist?
23. What should you do if you suspect carbon monoxide in your home?
24. How can you safely navigate icy sidewalks?
25. How can you make stairs safer to prevent falls?

Preparing Food

Complete the following tasks by describing the steps involved in preparing each item or meal. Say your answer aloud or write them on a separate piece of paper.

1. Describe the steps to prepare a turkey sandwich with lettuce and tomato.

2. Explain how to make a cup of hot cocoa with marshmallows.

3. Describe the process of making scrambled eggs with cheese.

4. How do you prepare a bowl of instant oatmeal with milk and honey?

5. Explain the steps for making a ham and cheese quesadilla.

6. Describe how to prepare a simple garden salad with dressing.

7. What are the steps to make a grilled chicken breast with vegetables?

8. Explain how to cook a frozen pizza in the oven.

9. Describe the process of making a cup of iced tea with lemon.

10. How do you prepare a bowl of spaghetti with marinara sauce?

11. Explain the steps for making a cup of instant noodles.

12. Describe how to cook a hamburger patty on a stovetop.

13. What are the steps to make a cheese and vegetable omelet?

14. Explain how to prepare a turkey and cranberry sandwich.

15. Describe the process of making a bowl of chicken noodle soup.

16. How do you make a peanut butter and banana sandwich?

17. Explain the steps for making a tuna salad with mayo and pickles.

18. Describe how to cook a frozen burrito in the microwave.

19. What are the steps to prepare a cup of instant coffee with cream?

20. Explain how to make a bowl of rice with soy sauce and vegetables.

21. Describe the process of making a fruit smoothie with yogurt.

22. How do you prepare a bowl of macaroni and cheese from a box?

23. Explain the steps for making a ham and pineapple pizza.

24. Describe how to cook a chicken drumstick in the oven.

25. What are the steps to make a bowl of fruit salad with assorted fruits?

Preparing Food

Complete the following tasks by describing the steps involved in preparing each item or meal. Say your answer aloud or write them on a separate piece of paper.

Describe all of the steps needed in order to prepare the following items.

1. Beef tacos with lettuce, cheese, and salsa.
2. A vegetable and cheese quesadilla.
3. Baked chicken breasts with a side of rice.
4. A classic Caesar salad with croutons and Caesar dressing.
5. Grilled shrimp with a garlic butter sauce.
6. A plate of spaghetti carbonara with bacon and Parmesan cheese.
7. A bowl of tomato soup with a grilled cheese sandwich.
8. A tuna melt sandwich with tomato and Swiss cheese.
9. A bowl of creamy macaroni and cheese.
10. A bowl of homemade chicken noodle soup.
11. A fruit salad with a variety of fresh fruits.
12. A pepperoni and mushroom pizza.
13. A classic club sandwich with turkey, bacon, lettuce, and tomato.
14. A bowl of vegetable curry with basmati rice.
15. A plate of chicken fajitas with peppers and onions.
16. A bowl of creamy tomato bisque with a grilled cheese sandwich.
17. A spinach and feta stuffed chicken breast.
18. A grilled steak with mashed potatoes and gravy.
19. A bowl of chicken and broccoli Alfredo pasta.
20. A homemade lasagna with layers of pasta, cheese, and meat sauce.
21. A plate of crispy fried chicken with coleslaw and biscuits.
22. A vegetarian sushi roll with avocado and cucumber.
23. A bowl of beef stew with carrots and potatoes.
24. A bowl of miso soup with tofu and seaweed.
25. A plate of barbecue ribs with cornbread and coleslaw.

Preparing Food

How would you prepare each of these meals? Write on a separate paper or say aloud.

1. What is the first step in boiling pasta?

2. How do you know when a cake is done baking?

3. What ingredients are needed to make scrambled eggs?

4. Describe the steps to make a sandwich.

5. What safety precautions should you take when using a stove?

6. How long should you wash vegetables before cooking?

7. What is the difference between baking and grilling chicken?

8. How do you prepare rice?

9. What are three essential tools needed for baking a pie?

10. How can you tell if meat is cooked properly?

11. Describe the process of making a salad.

12. What are common ingredients in a vegetable stir-fry?

13. How do you measure ingredients for a recipe?

14. What are the steps to make homemade soup?

15. How do you safely cut vegetables?

16. What temperature should you set an oven for baking bread?

17. How do you prevent food from sticking to a pan?

18. What ingredients are in a smoothie?

19. How do you clean up after cooking a meal?

20. What is the process for marinating meat?

21. How do you make a cup of coffee?

22. What is needed to set a table for dinner?

23. How do you store leftovers?

24. What are the steps to make pancakes?

25. How do you check if an egg is fresh?

Preparing Food

How would you prepare each of these meals? Write on a separate paper or say aloud.

1. How do you knead dough for bread, and why is this step important?
2. What are the key differences in ingredients between a quiche and an omelette?
3. Describe the process of blanching vegetables.
4. How do you make a reduction sauce?
5. What are the essential steps in preparing and cooking a roast?
6. How do you determine the right amount of seasoning for a dish?
7. Describe the technique of sautéing vegetables.
8. What are the steps to prepare a homemade pizza, including the crust?
9. How do you properly thaw frozen meat?
10. What is the process for filleting a fish?
11. Describe how to prepare a vegan meal.
12. What are the steps for baking a multi-layer cake?
13. How do you prepare and cook food using a slow cooker?
14. What techniques are involved in making homemade pasta?
15. How do you balance flavors in a dish?
16. Describe the process of fermenting vegetables.
17. How do you prepare a meal using only raw ingredients?
18. What are the key steps in making a soufflé?
19. How do you grill different types of vegetables?
20. What is the technique for making a clear broth?
21. How do you make a meal with five ingredients or less?
22. Describe how to prepare a traditional dish from another culture.
23. How do you adjust a recipe to make it healthier?
24. What are the steps to organize a meal plan for a week?
25. How do you make homemade ice cream without an ice cream maker?

Temporal Awareness

Answer these questions about time. Use a separate piece of paper or say aloud.

1. How long does it typically take to shower and get dressed?

2. What is the best time of day to go grocery shopping, and why?

3. How do you plan a day when you have an appointment at 3 PM?

4. How long should you brush your teeth, and why?

5. Estimate how long it takes to cook and eat breakfast.

6. What time of year do you change the clocks for daylight saving time?

7. How do you determine the time needed to travel to a new place?

8. Describe a good bedtime routine and how long it should take.

9. How long does it take to do laundry, including washing and drying?

10. Estimate the time needed to clean a room.

11. How often should you water plants, and at what time of day?

12. What is the best time to exercise, considering your daily routine?

13. How do you manage time when cooking a meal with multiple dishes?

14. Describe the process of planning a weekend trip.

15. How long does a typical work or school day last?

16. How often should you check your email, and why?

17. What is the ideal frequency and duration for grocery shopping?

18. How do you plan your day around a favorite TV show's airing time?

19. Estimate how long it takes to read a chapter of a book.

20. How do you decide when to start preparing for a holiday?

21. What is a reasonable time to spend on social media each day?

22. How do you plan a schedule for regular exercise?

23. How long should you wait after eating before going to bed?

24. Estimate the time needed to visit a doctor, including travel.

25. How do you manage time when you have multiple tasks in one day?

Temporal Awareness

Answer these questions about time. Use a separate piece of paper or say aloud.

1. What time of day do you usually eat breakfast?

2. How long does it take to brush your teeth?

3. When is the best time to go to bed at night?

4. How long does a typical meal last?

5. What time do you usually wake up in the morning?

6. Estimate how long it takes to get dressed.

7. When do you usually have lunch?

8. How long should you wash your hands?

9. What is your favorite time of day, and why?

10.   How long does it take to make a bed?

11.   When is a good time to do homework or read a book?

12.   Estimate how long a TV show episode lasts.

13.   When do you usually have dinner?

14.   How long does it take to take a short walk?

15.   What time of day do you prefer for exercise?

16.   Estimate how long it takes to write a letter or an email.

17.   When is a good time to call a friend or family member?

18.   How long does a typical shopping trip take?

19.   What time of year is your birthday?

20.   How long does it take to clean a small mess in the kitchen?

21.   When is the best time to water plants?

22.   Estimate the duration of a car or bus ride to a familiar place.

23.   When do you usually do laundry?

24.   How long does it take to pack a bag for a day trip?

25.   What time of year do the leaves change color?

Spatial Awareness

Follow the directions for each task involving spatial awareness:

Task 1:

In the upper-left square, draw a triangle.

In the upper-right square, write the letter "A."

In the lower-left square, draw a smiley face.

In the lower-right square, write your initials.

Task 2:

In the upper-left square, draw a star.

In the upper-right square, write the number "7."

In the lower-left square, draw a heart.

In the lower-right square, write the word "sun."

Task 3:

In the upper-left square, draw a house.

In the upper-right square, write the letter "B."

In the lower-left square, draw a tree.

In the lower-right square, write the word "moon."

Task 4:

In the upper-left square, draw a car.

In the upper-right square, write the number "3."

In the lower-left square, draw a flower.

In the lower-right square, write the word "star."

Spatial Awareness

Follow the directions for each task involving spatial awareness:

Task 5:

In the upper-left square, draw a sun.

In the upper-right square, write the letter "C."

In the lower-left square, draw a cloud.

In the lower-right square, write your favorite number.

Task 6:

In the upper-left square, draw a boat.

In the upper-right square, write the number "5."

In the lower-left square, draw a fish.

In the lower-right square, write the word "bird."

Task 7:

In the upper-left square, draw a mountain.

In the upper-right square, write the letter "D."

In the lower-left square, draw a river.

In the lower-right square, write the word "ocean."

Task 8:

In the upper-left square, draw a house.

In the upper-right square, write the number "8."

In the lower-left square, draw a tree.

In the lower-right square, write the word "flower."